デザインやクリエイティブ関連の仕事に
少しでも携わる人は、業務のユニークさ、楽しさ、
奥深さを日々味わっていることでしょう。
そしてどのような職種でも、
またどんな立場にある人であっても、時には悩み、
自問自答しながらプロジェクトに
向き合っているに違いありません。

この本は、仕事の合間や通勤・移動時間に
読んでいただければと思います。
建築設計、アートディレクション、家具制作、
不動産コンサルティング、写真撮影、PR、照明デザイン、
ファッションデザイン、フラワーデコレーション、編集。
デザインやクリエイティブ業界の第一線で活躍する
10人のエキスパートの、仕事をするうえで鍵となる
考えやアイデア、アドバイスが並んでいます。
経験から紡ぎだされた、含蓄のある言葉の数々が
凝縮されているのです。

この本には章や分類はありません。
好きなところを開き、あなたが今求めている
言葉に出会ってください。
そこに込められた知恵によって、今のプロジェクトを
より良くするヒントが得られ、
あなたの未来に確かな導きと
豊かな彩りがもたらされることでしょう。

腕のいい
デザイナーが
必ずやっている
仕事のルール125

1

番最初に
こだわろう

Be the first to get there

後に続くのではなく、切り拓く人になろう。トップという1番の座にはなかなか上がれないかもしれないが、「初」という1番につくことはできる。最初というのはそれだけで目立つ。「誰もやらないなら、自分がやる」というスタンスでいこう。

Don't be someone who just picks up the slack – be the guy who blazes the trail. You might not succeed in becoming the absolute top dog in your field, but you can be the "first" to get there. Just being the first to have tried something will make you stand out. Tell yourself, "I'll do it myself since nobody else will".

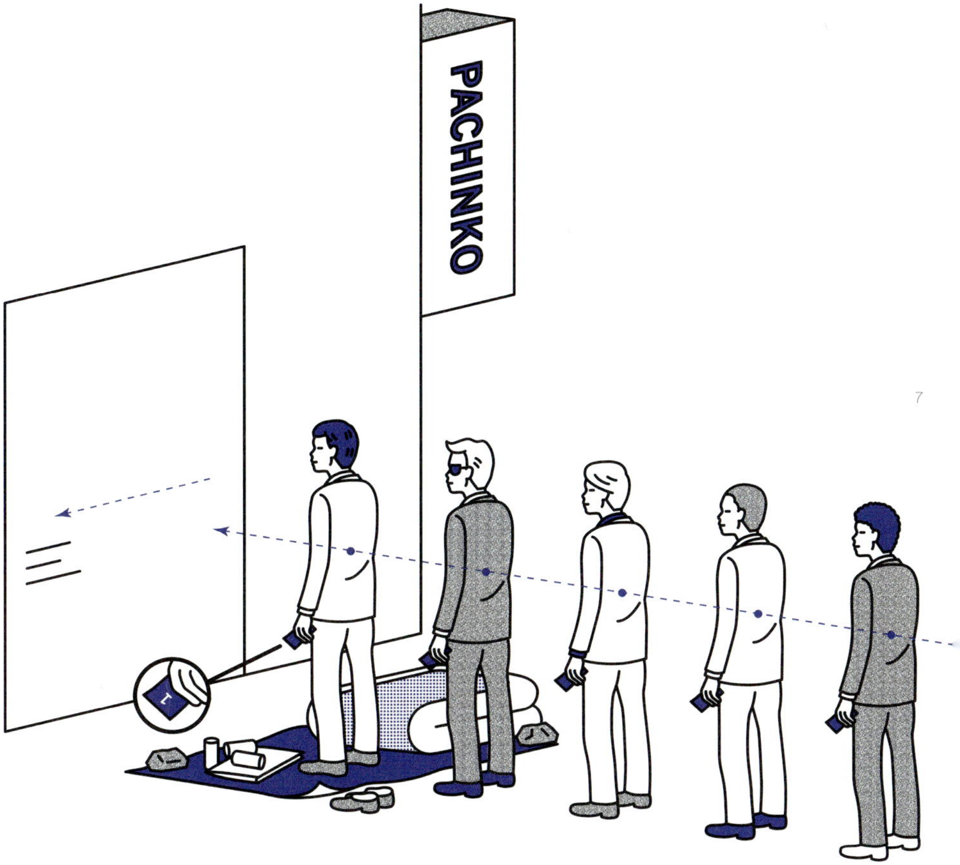
PACHINKO

START
根拠のない自信をもつ

Have groundless self-confidence

GOAL

思い切って結論ありきの話をしてみる。みんながぎょっとしてもかまわない。そこにたどり着くようにルートを考え、状況に合わせて登り続ければよい。

Try saying something sweeping and conclusive once in a while. Who cares if you end up startling a few people? All you need to do then is to think about how you're going to reach that conclusion, and play the game according to the circumstances.

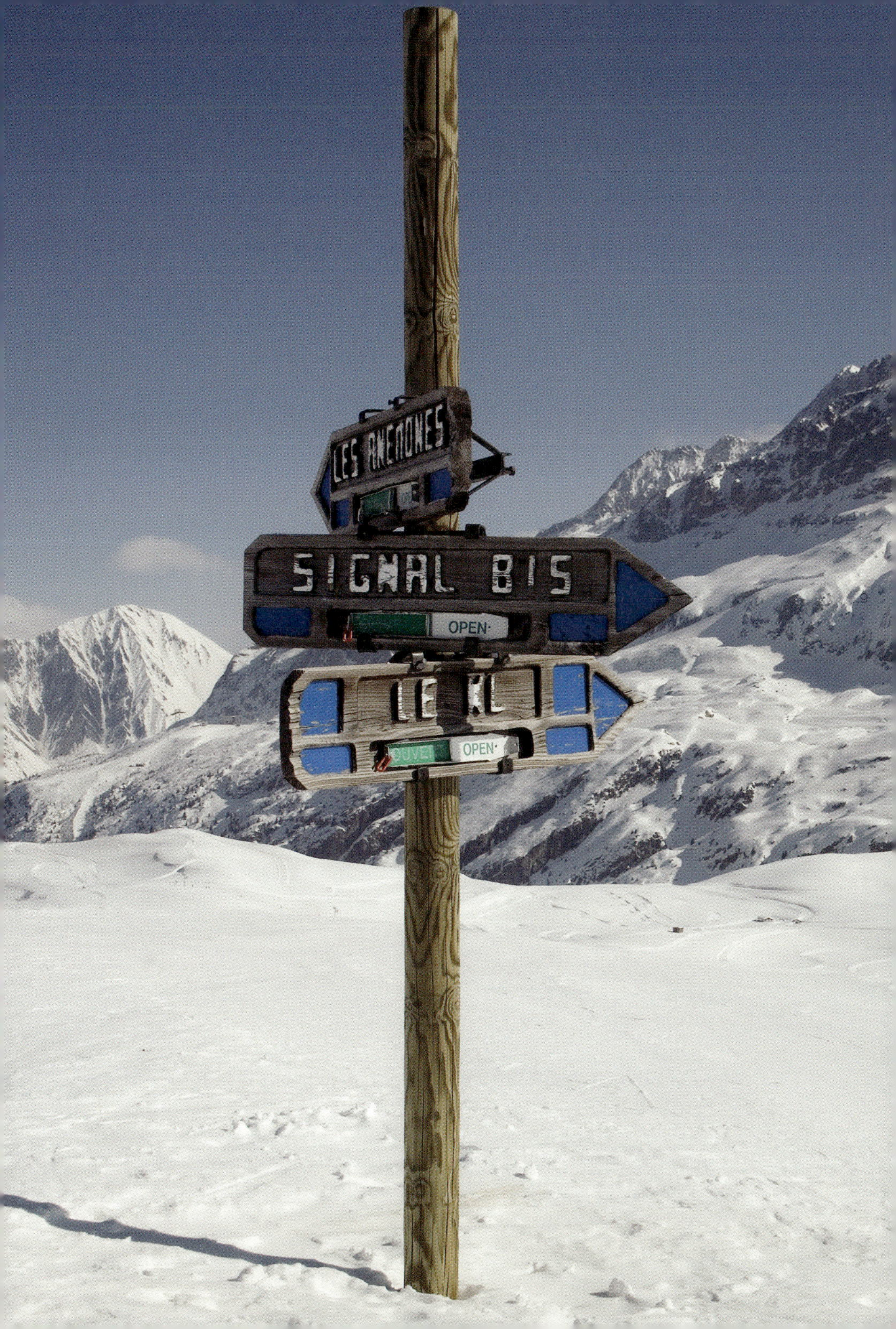
LES ANEMONES
SIGNAL BIS
OPEN
LE KL
OPEN

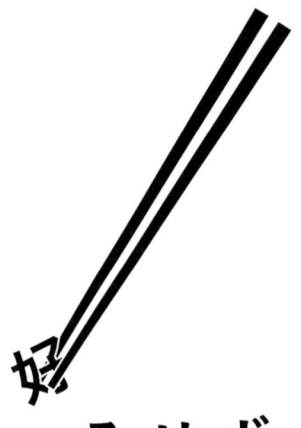

選り好みせず
何でも味わおう

Don't be picky-
get a taste of everything

偶然なのか・必然なのか。突然やってくるチャンスにどう向き合うか。「ノーサンキュー（＝要りません）」からは何も生まれない。デザイナーは職業というより、生き方に近い。日々さまざまな価値観に触れて、選り好みせず何でも味わう余裕をもちたい。結果うまくいかなくても、すべてが大きな1つのデザインフェーズだと思えばいい。人生をデザインしているつもりで…

Do things happen by coincidence, or out of necessity? How should you tackle an opportunity that suddenly comes your way? Nothing will come out of a "no, thank you". Design is a way of life, rather than an occupation — they set out to make sure they have the time and freedom to sample a little bit of everything that life has to offer them, without being too picky. Even if the end result doesn't go the way you planned, just treat the whole process as a single, massive phase, just as if you'd intended to design your own life…

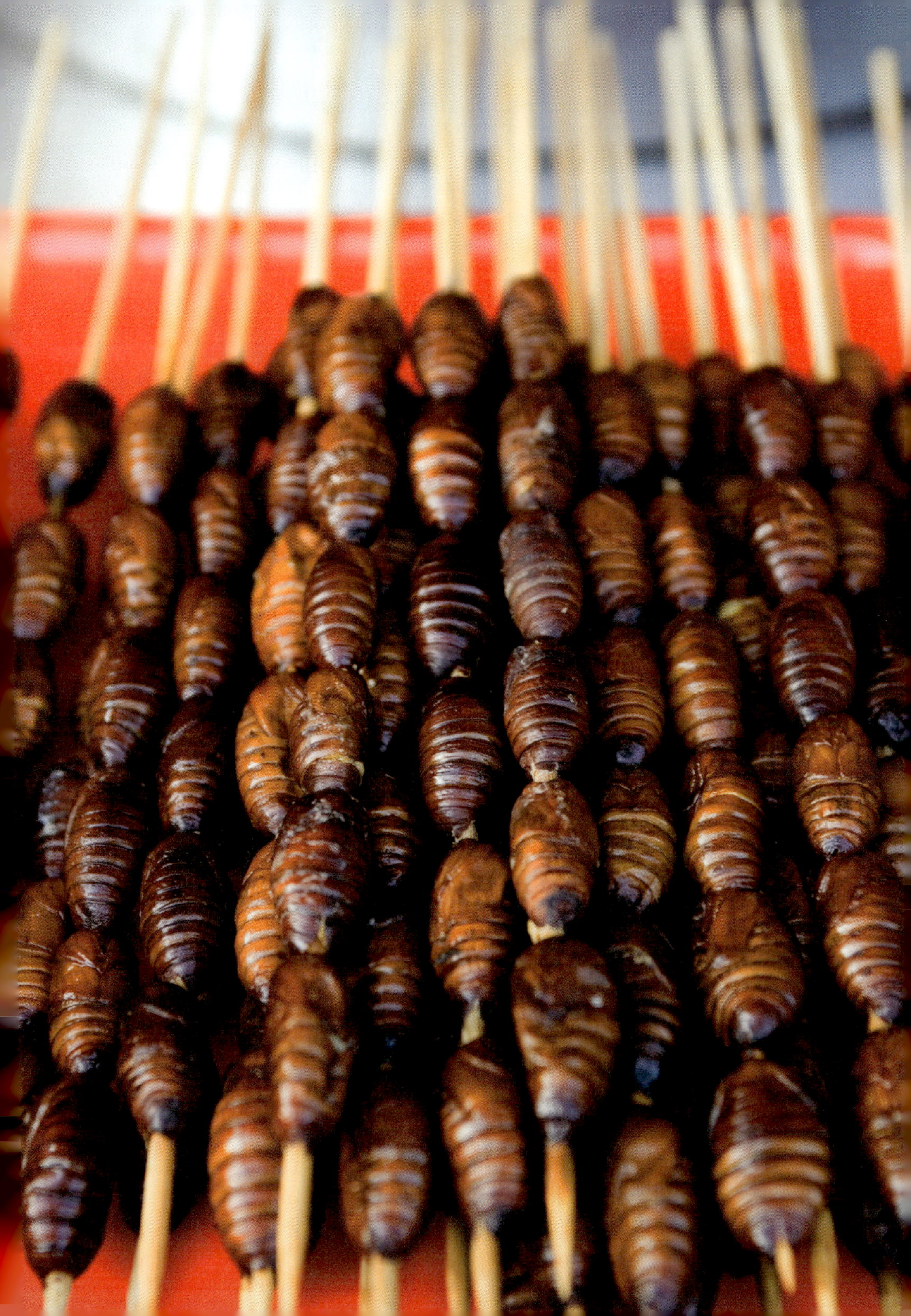

時間に間に合わせよう

Start → Fix

Meet those deadlines

デザインの仕事は限られた平等の時間のなかで、どれだけの成果を残せるかという創造のゲームである。いかなる妙案が生まれようと、時間に間に合わなければ残念ながら零点である。「もう少し時間があればできた」と言い訳をするスタッフがいるが、過信してはならない。仕事に取り組む根本姿勢や時間へのだらしなさは、明確にデザインに表れる。

Design is a sort of creative game where people compete to see how much of a lasting impact they can achieve within the same limited span of time. No matter how amazing your idea is, no points are awarded if you don't make it in time. You can't place too much good faith in staff who make excuses like "I would've been able to do it if I had more time". Your basic attitude towards work and sense of discipline show up very clearly in the designs you produce.

メロス!!

予算を疑え

Be suspicious about budgeting issues

「本当にここにお金をかける必要があるか」を熟考することがデザインにつながる。お金があれば、よいデザインができるわけではない。むしろその反対である。

Giving serious thought to whether you really need to spend money on one thing or another is an essential aspect of design. You're not going to end up with a good design just because you have the money — it's actually the opposite.

おさわりパブ

熟女

90分
4,000円

(お1人様のご料金)
飲み放題
(ビール・ウンサワー)

すでにある波に乗れ

Ride the waves
that are already there

自分がつくり出す流れよりも、世のなかにある流れのほうが大きく速い。最初に体力を使って無理に自分で波を立てようと意気込むのではなく、すでにある波をよく観察して分別しよう。よい波をうまくつかまえて流れに乗り、そのなかで自分の流れをつくり出すほうが簡単である。

The trends and currents that are already out there in the world flow much faster than anything you might create on your own. Rather than expending all that energy and getting all passionate about starting the next big thing on your own, study what's already out there, and separate the wheat from the chaff. It's easier to get into the game if you latch onto a wave and ride the current for a while before striking out on your own.

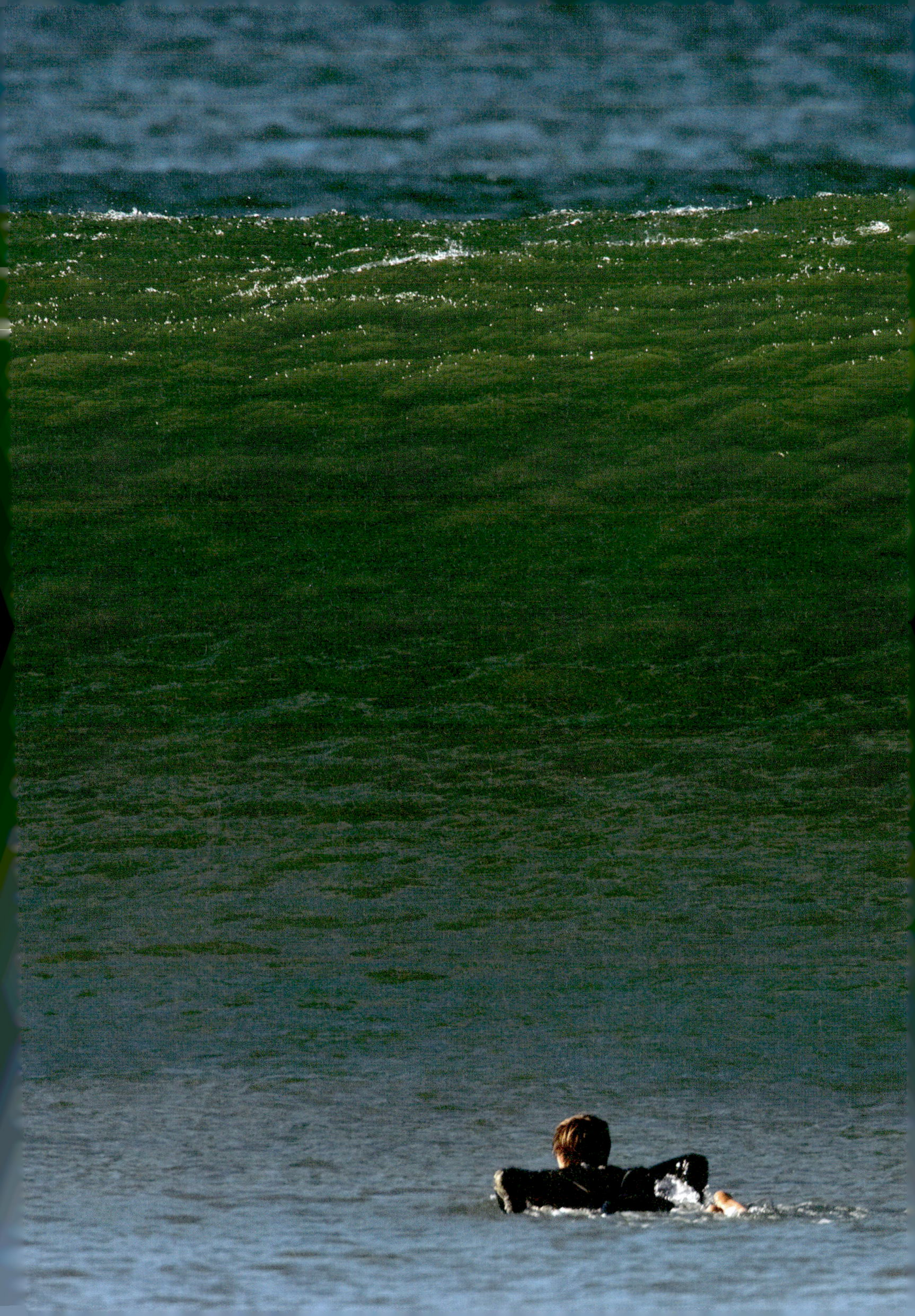

Step up

ステップアップしよう

自分でデザイン業を始めたら、まずは人に見せられる実績を何としてでもつくろう。それから自分の欲しいデザイン料を示せる自分を目指そう。仕事の数が充実してきたら、仲間を増やして高くても頼まれる状況を目指そう。最後は自分がしたい仕事を選べ、自分の時間をつくれるようになれたら最高だね。

Once your design career has begun, work hard to make achievements that can be shown to others. Then pursue a status that allows you to offer your desired design fee. When you gain enough work, increase the size of your staff and aim for a status where clients offer you jobs for high fees. It would be wonderful to be able to choose work that you want to do, and to create free time at the end.

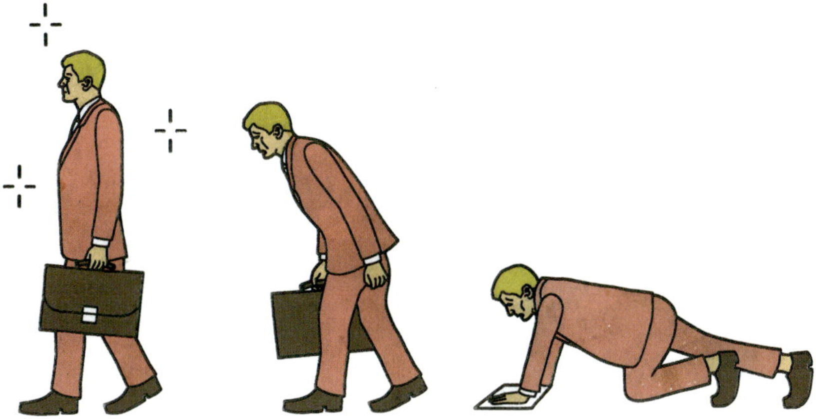

粘れ

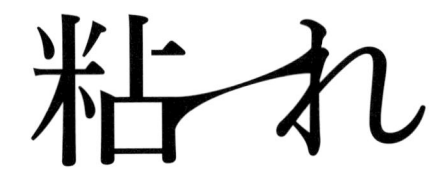

Stick with it

限られた時間のなかで粘り、粘り、ひたすら粘る。長いプロセスのなかで、真の答えはその最終局面のほんの一瞬に宿るので、一瞬たりとも気を抜いてはならない。しつこく粘ることでデザインが完成する。ちなみに、デザインとは粘ることだから体力が必要。自分の事務所では「体力はありますか？」と聞いて「自信があります！」と答える人間しか採用しない。

Persevere, persevere, and then persevere some more within a limited span of time. The real answer can be found only in a single moment at the very last stage of a long process, so you have to be sure not to slacken for even an instant. Designs come to completion by sticking hard and fast and not letting go. It's a demanding, physical operation. At my own firm, we only hire people who are confident about their own strength and physical health.

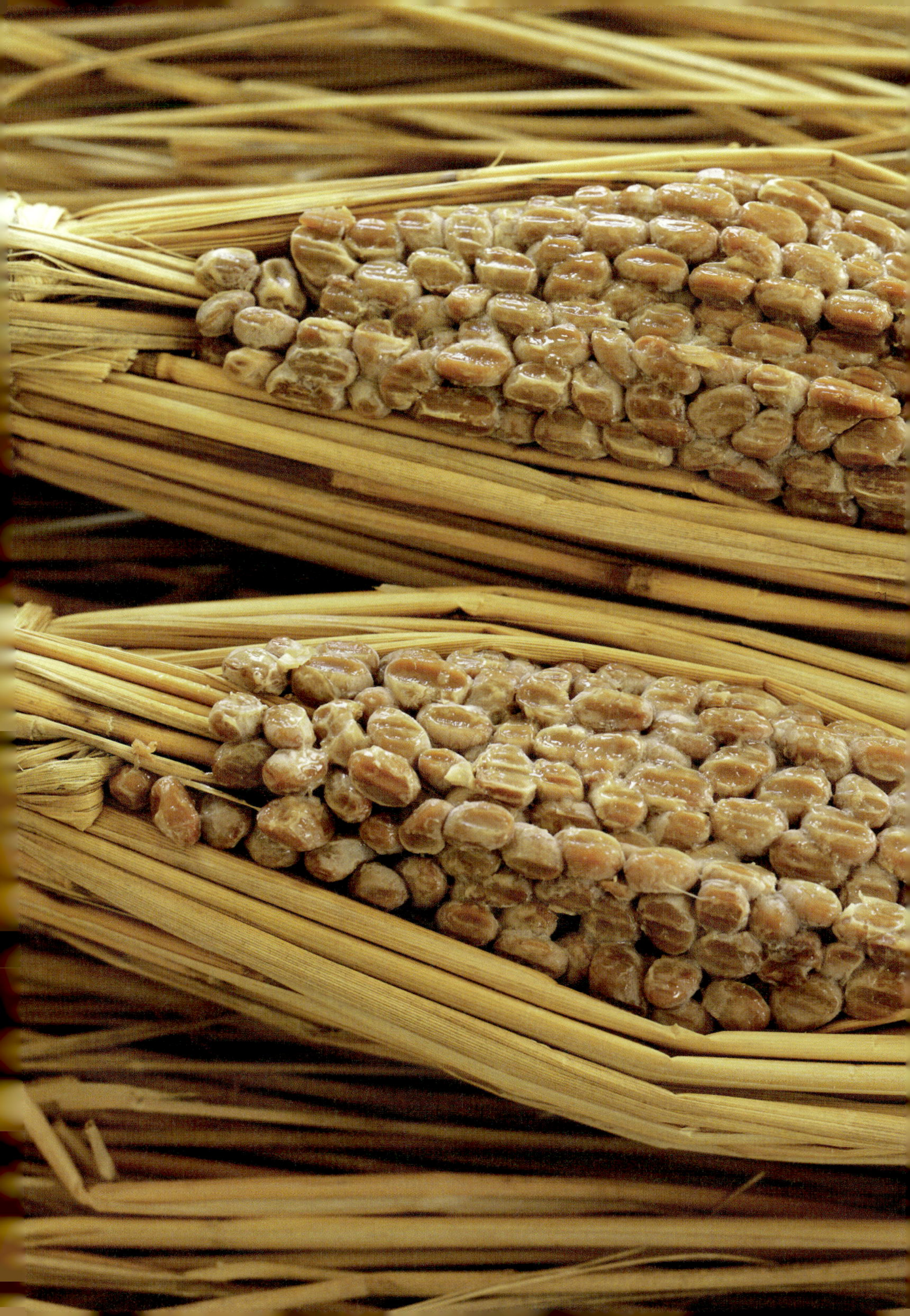

業界を

遠くで見たり

近くで見たりしよう

Look at your industry
both up close and from afar

業界の常識は、一般には通用しないこともある。また、一般常識と思っていることでも、特定の業界ではそうでない場合もある。常に両方の目をもつことが大切。「もし自分が製作側だったら」「もし自分がお客さん側だったら」と、行ったり来たりして考えることで擦り合わせができるようになり、うまく運ぶことも多い。

What might pass for common knowledge in one industry sometimes doesn't apply at all to normal life. Similarly, even what one assumes to be common practice may not hold in certain specific contexts. Remember to always look at things from both these perspectives. By imagining yourself to be in the position of the creator, or the client, and going back and forth between these viewpoints, you'll be able to overlay one on top of the other and everything will work out well.

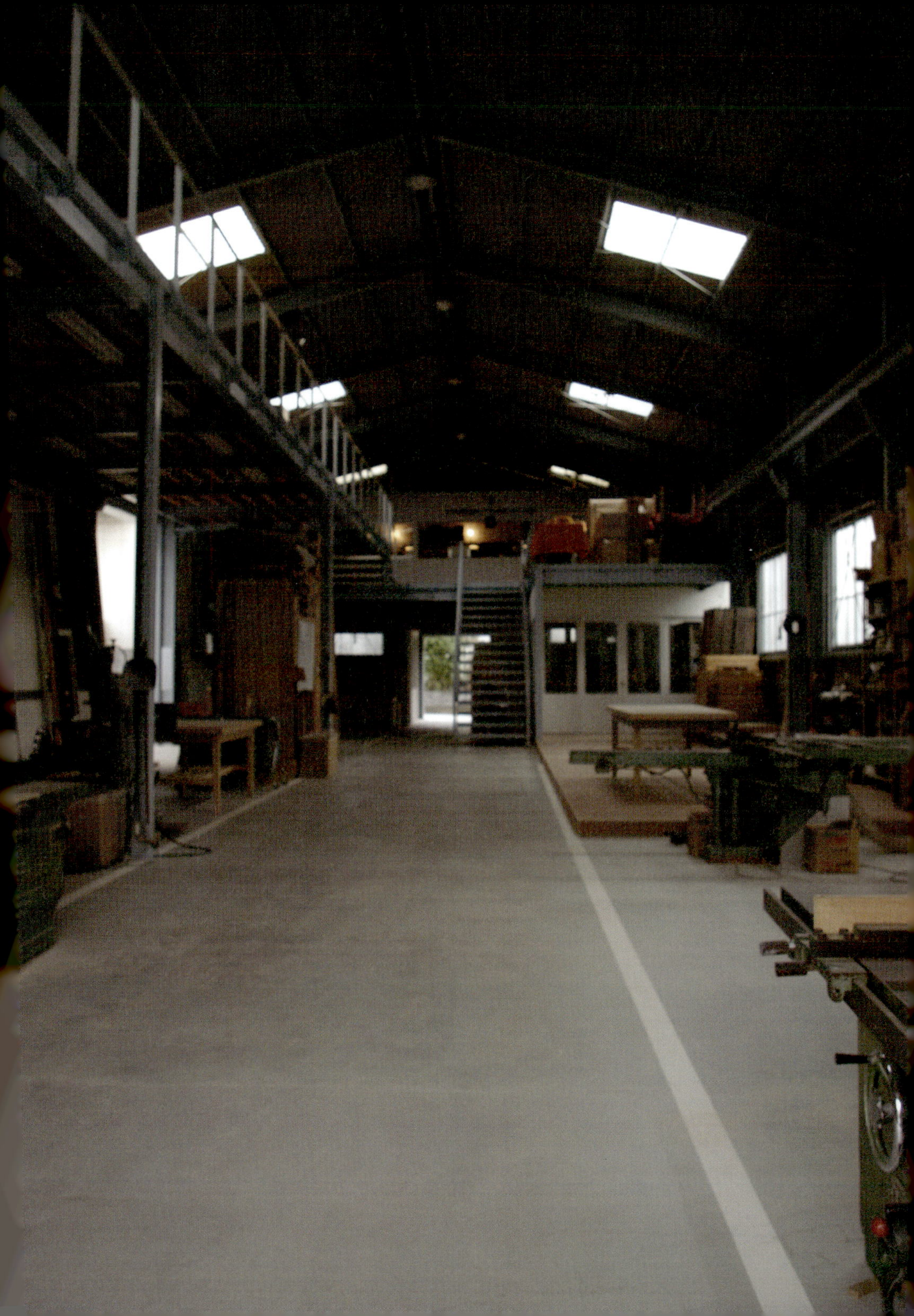

Set a target

ターゲットを定めよう

デザインはアートと異なり、相手に合わせてモノづくりをする。自分のデザインの特徴をよく知り、そのデザインが最も受け入れられるクライアント層をターゲットにすることが大切だ。違う層とも仕事をしたければ、デザインの幅も広げなければならない。常に戦略を持つことはビジネスの基本である。

Unlike art, a design is created depending on clients. It's important to be familiar with the characteristics of your design, and pursue client groups who most accept your designs. To work with other groups, diversification of your design range is required. Having a strategy is one of the basics of business.

25

伸び代の可能性を示そう

Show your potential
for growth

カラーがあること自体は悪いことではないが、伸び悩む可能性は極端に増す。一方で、必要な色に染まることのできるフレキシビリティには可能性を感じるものだ。若い人には経験がない代わりに、伸び代がある。伸び代の可能性＝才能にかけてみたいと思うときに、先輩は手を差し伸べ、クライアントは依頼を検討する。知らないことを恐れず謙虚に学び、伸び代の可能性を示していこう。

Having a distinct, fixed quality to your work is not in itself a bad thing, but the room for growth in someone who's still inexperienced is much, much greater. In contrast, there's lots of potential in a flexible attitude that can adapt as necessary. What young people lack in experience, they make up for in terms of potential. When juniors decide to develop this potential and talent, their seniors ought to step in and help, and clients should hire them for jobs. Don't be afraid of what you don't know, learn humbly, and make that potential flourish.

27

メイン
でも

サブでも
あれ

Play both the lead
and supporting roles

プロジェクトによって自身の役割をあえて変えることで、客観性は獲得できる。そのためにはさまざまなジャンルの仕事を大勢の人々と行う必要がある。同じ人と決まった仕事しかしなければ変化や広がり、柔軟な発想はそれ以上生まれない。メインとサブ、両方の役割が演じられるようになれば本物だ。

You learn to become more objective by assuming different roles depending on the project. In order to pull this off, you need to work with lots of people on all sorts of different projects. If you only work on set projects with the same group of people, you're not going to gain breadth, accomplish change, or get a more flexible and versatile handle on things. The ultimate goal is to become able to play both the main role and the supporting one.

29

期待されていることを考えよう

Think about what's expected of you

デザイナーが依頼を受けるとき、カラーがはっきりしているベテランデザイナーの場合は、その路線に沿ったアウトプットが期待されていることが多い。一方で、経験のないデザイナーの場合はどうだろう。デザイナーは、自分が何を期待されているのかを考えてもよいだろう。それが「勢い」なのか「イレギュラー」なのか「新しい感覚」なのか。それを踏まえてデザインするだけで、無駄なやり取りが減るかもしれない。

When veteran designers accept commissions for work, clients often expect results that mirror the style or idiom that those designers have become known for. What about designers with no experience, though? Maybe designers should also think hard about what's expected of them – is it energy, unpredictability, or freshness? Just by going about your work with this in mind, you might be able to rid yourself of time-wasting, unproductive exchanges.

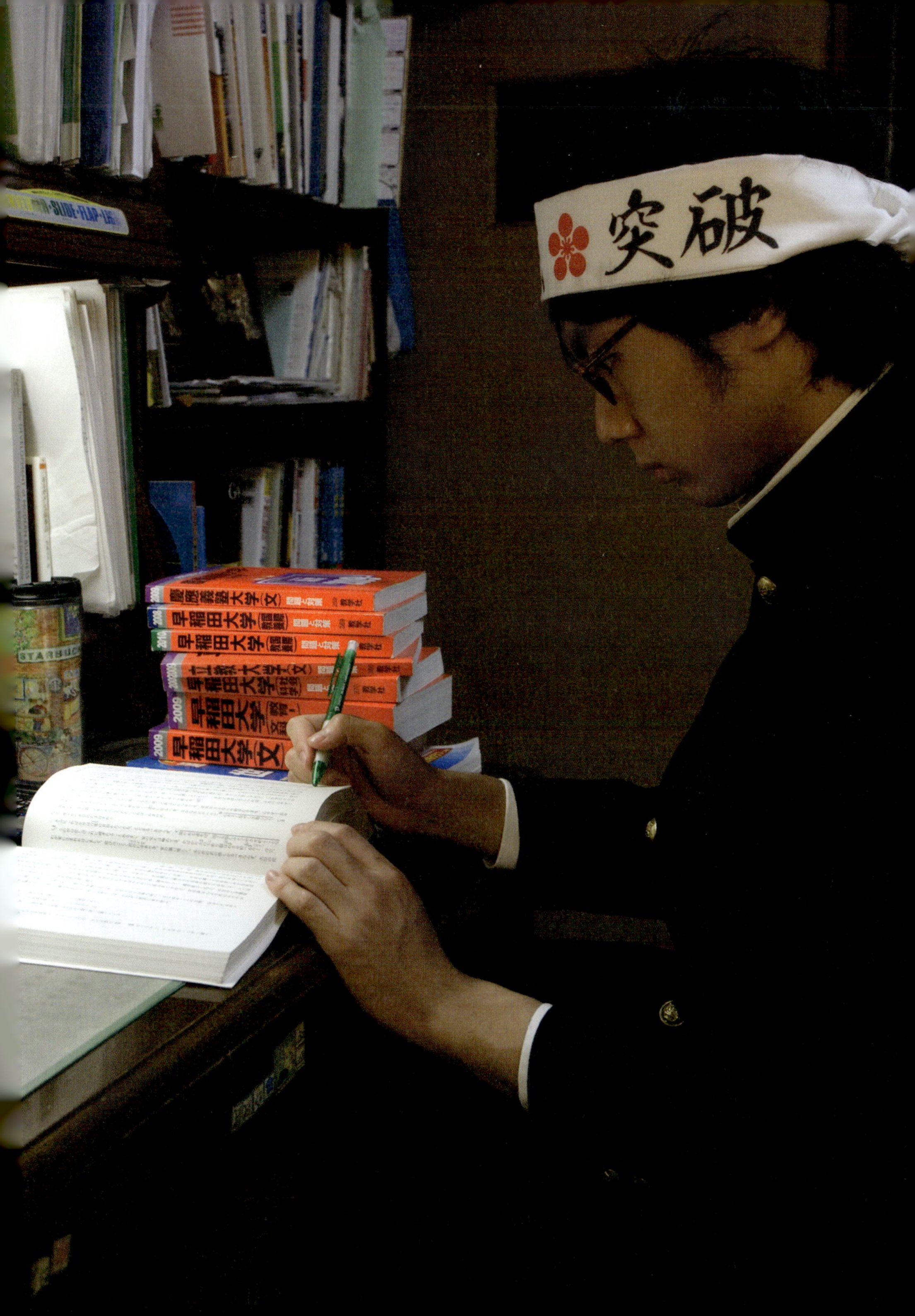
突破
早稲田大学 文

```
              idea
               ·
   価値
visual ·············|············· brand
               :
               :
              work
```

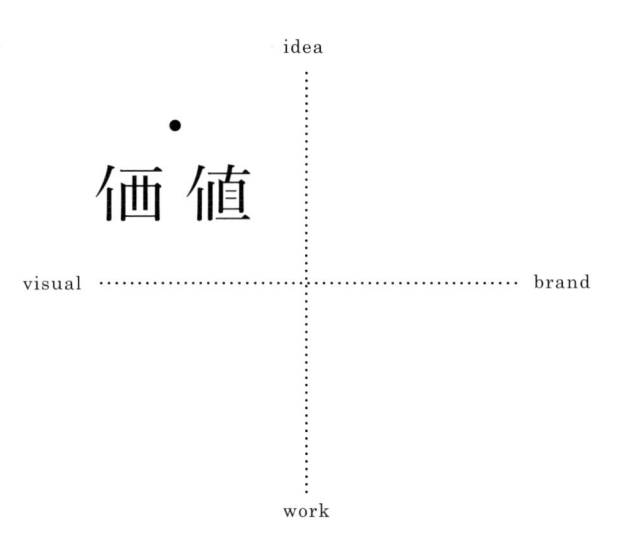

の居場所を考えよう

Consider where the value exists

クライアントが支払うデザイン料は、何に対して払ってくれているのか考えてみよう。労働力？　ブランド？　アイデア？　美しいビジュアル？　相手が認めている価値と、自分たちが求めたい価値とがずれていると、どこかでひずみが生じる。逆に合っていれば、お互いのビジネスを最大化できるはずだ。

Think about what the client pays for with the design fee, such as labor, brands, ideas, or beautiful visuals. If there is a gap between the values that the client recognizes and the values you want to pursue, the relationship will be distorted at some point. Conversely, if your values match, you should be able to maximize each other's business.

33

volume

量をこなし

quality

質を上げよう

Boost quality by increasing volume

質量転化の法則。さまざまなバリエーションの仕事を同時にこなすことで、デザインの創造力は飛躍的に拡大する。直線的に攻めたり、迂回したり、引き返したりするなかで、経験が積み重なり、大きな山も攻略できるようになる。プロジェクトのヒントはほかのプロジェクトに隠されているケースも多い。一見無駄なことのなかにこそ問題解決の糸口があり、遠回りするなかで新しい景色が見える。たとえばジャグリングのように１度に多くが動いているダイナミックな状態こそが、新しいものが生まれる最良のシチュエーションである。

Big masses tend to undergo a transformation. By pursuing all sorts of varied projects at the same time, your design creativity is going to expand dramatically. Over the course of trying direct, head-on approaches, making detours, or retracing your steps, you accumulate experience and become able to tackle even the most daunting obstacles. The key to one project is often hidden within another. Hints to solving a particular problem can sometimes lie precisely within something that seems utterly useless. Going around in circles and taking the long way around can reveal a new vista. The dynamism to be found in many parts being activated at the same time, just like juggling, is the best situation in terms of making new discoveries.

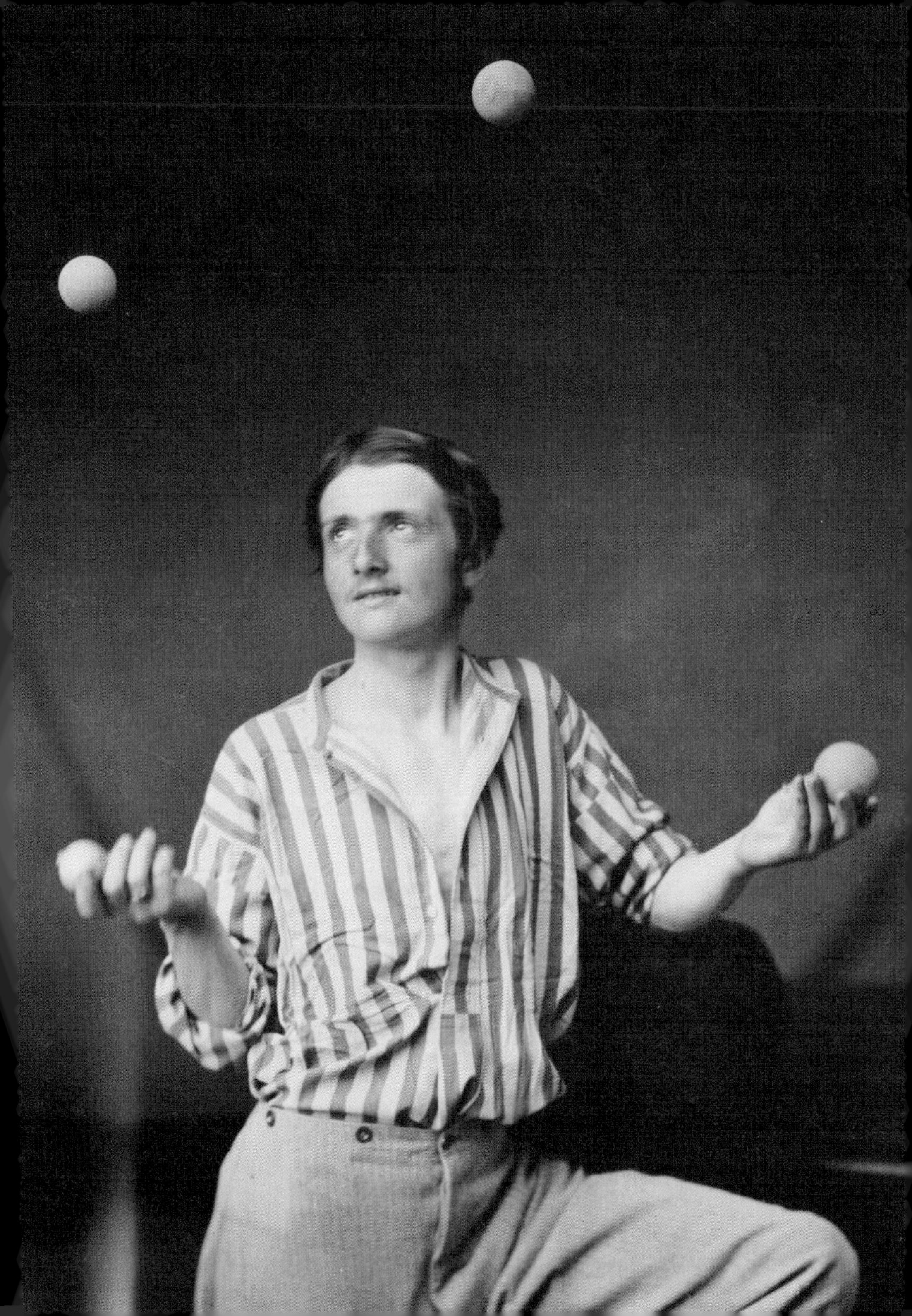

異なるアドバイスがあっても試してみよう

Try it and see, even if someone tells you otherwise

ある先輩から指示を受け、やり方まで教わる。それを進めていると、ほかの先輩からこうやったほうがよいと声をかけられ、しばし困る。異なる2つのアドバイス。右向け右、左向け左。やらないわけにはいかない。2度手間にはなるが、そこは我慢をし、時間を圧縮して作業を進める。なにしろ2種類の手法が手に入るのだから。こういうふうに考えても、悪くはなさそうだ。

So one of your seniors gives you instructions, and even shows you how to get something done. When you do as you've been told, though, someone else tells you that it should be done his way, which confuses you. You need to take a position, and choose if you're going to take your cue from your left or your right. Maybe it's going to take you twice the time and effort, but suck it up and get on with your work as efficiently as you can. Ultimately, you're going to learn two ways of getting things done, so just go for it. You could do a lot worse.

ANGEL

DEVIL

同じ前を向こう

Keep your eyes trained on the same target

クライアントとデザイナーは、ついついガッツリと向かい合って、顔色を見ながらの駆け引きになりがち。発想を変えて、向かい合うのではなく同じ方向を向いてみよう。一緒になって同じ方向に向かって歩いている「感じ」にできたら、しめたモノ！　クライアントは敵ではなく、同志に変わる。

Designers and clients tend to be too uptight when they meet, haggling with each other while trying to figure out what the other is thinking. Instead of being so high-strung and confrontational, let's try seeing eye to eye, and look in the same direction. Once it feels as if we're headed in the same destination, it's a done deal. Don't think of your client as your enemy, but as someone on your own team.

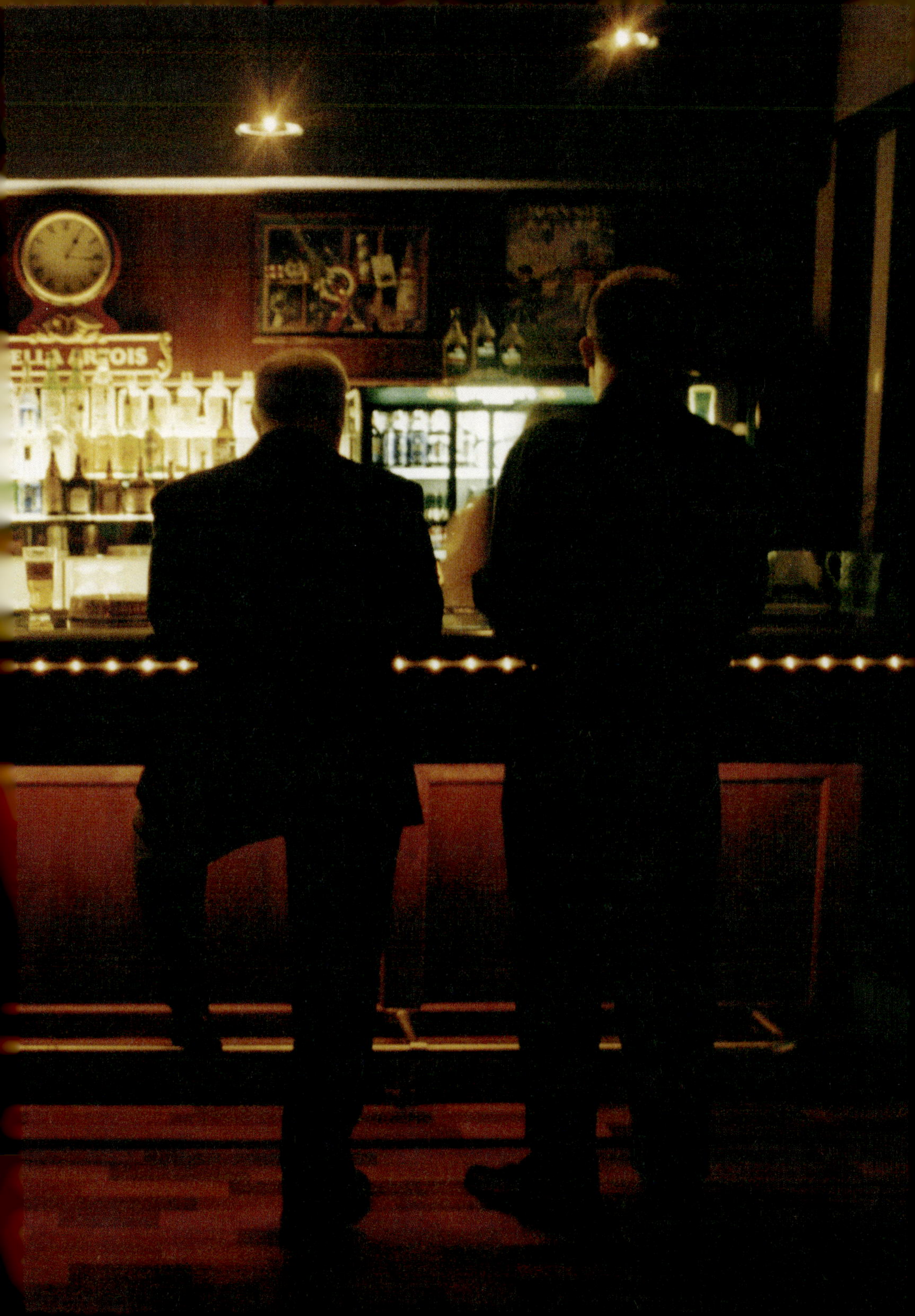

契約の流れで危険性を測ろう

Use the contract-signing
process to measure the risk

契約を結ばないクライアントは基本的に、貴方を信用してないか、だまそうとしているかのどちらかだ。本気で依頼する気があれば、契約を結ぶことに何ら障害はないはずだ。また、契約すると言ったのに実際には契約がスムーズに進まないときは危険信号だ。デザインはお互いの信用関係が成立していることが絶対条件。すぐに手を止め、相手をけん制しよう。時には手を引く勇気を持とう。契約していないということは、こちらも自由なのだから。

Basically, if a client does not sign a contract, they do not trust you or they are trying to deceive you. If they truly intended to offer you a job, no obstruction should exist to signing a contract. It is a danger sign when the client agrees to make a contract but the contract process does not proceed smoothly. An absolute requirement for design is the establishment of a mutual-trust relationship. Stop immediately and warn the client. Sometimes having the courage to walk away is required. Having no contract means you are also free.

婚 姻 届

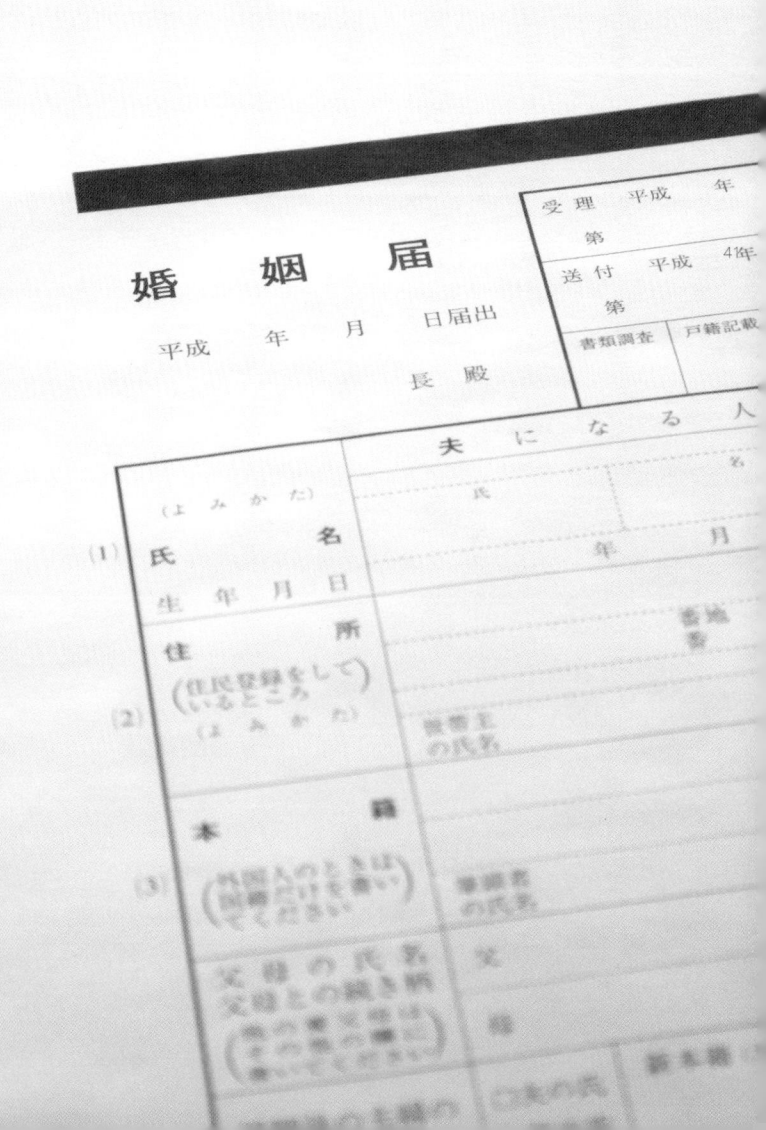

平成　年　月　日届出

　　　長　殿

受理	平成　年
	第
送付	平成 4 年
	第
書類調査	戸籍記載

夫 に な る 人

	（よみかた）	氏　　　　名
(1)	氏　　　　名	年　　　月
	生 年 月 日	
	住　　　　所	番地 番
(2)	（住民登録をして いるところ）	
	（よみかた）	世帯主 の氏名
	本　　　　籍	
(3)	（外国人のときは 国籍だけを書い てください）	筆頭者 の氏名
	父母の氏名 父母との続き柄	父
	（他の養父母は その他の欄に 書いてください）	母
		ご夫の氏 新本籍

理解者を増やしていこう

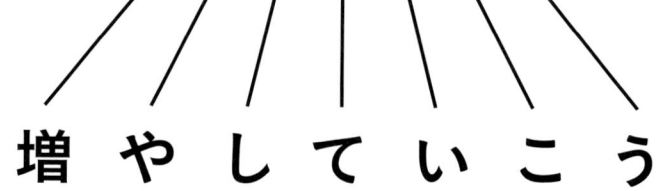

Get to know more people who understand you

自分のやりたい仕事をやりたいなら、1人ずつ周りに理解者を増やせばいい。とにかく想いを伝え、考えを述べ、意義を示し、そして誰よりもそのことについての愛があり、長けていることを証明すること。自分1人でできることは限られている。ボスや仕事仲間、クライアントと夢を共有する。共通の目標をもち、そこに辿り着くためのマインドがあればこそ、成し得ることが格段に増えていく。

If you want to do the jobs you want, start by getting to know people who understand what you're about, one by one. More than anything else, you need to communicate what you're thinking, describe your thought processes, demonstrate what you mean — and prove that nobody has a greater passion and knowledge than you do for the subject in question. There's a limit to what a single person can do. Share your dreams with your boss, colleagues, and clients. When you share common objectives and have a frame of mind that will lead you to accomplish them that, the things you'll be capable of are going to increase dramatically.

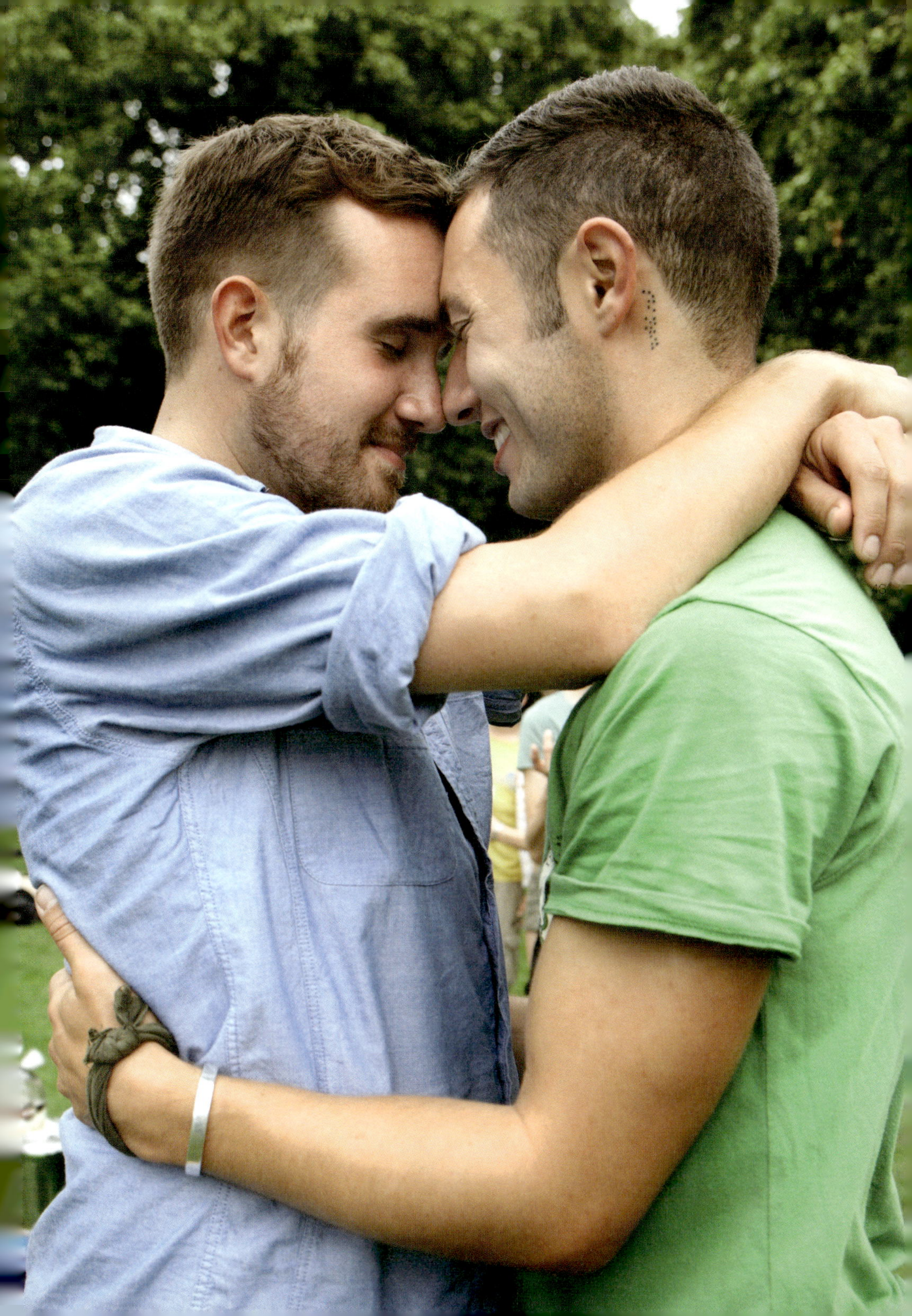

タイミング》
《がすべて

Timing is everything 》》

よいデザインが注目を集めるカギは、タイミングをつかむことにある。PRが効果を発揮するのもほんの一瞬。いくらよい写真や図面などの資料があっても、ニュースになる新鮮なうちにPRをしなければ意味がない。

The key to getting a good piece of design noticed has everything to do with the right timing. Even an effective PR campaign only works for an extremely brief window of time. No matter how amazing your photography, diagrams, and other materials are, they won't mean anything unless you get your PR out there while it's still fresh and can make a good news item.

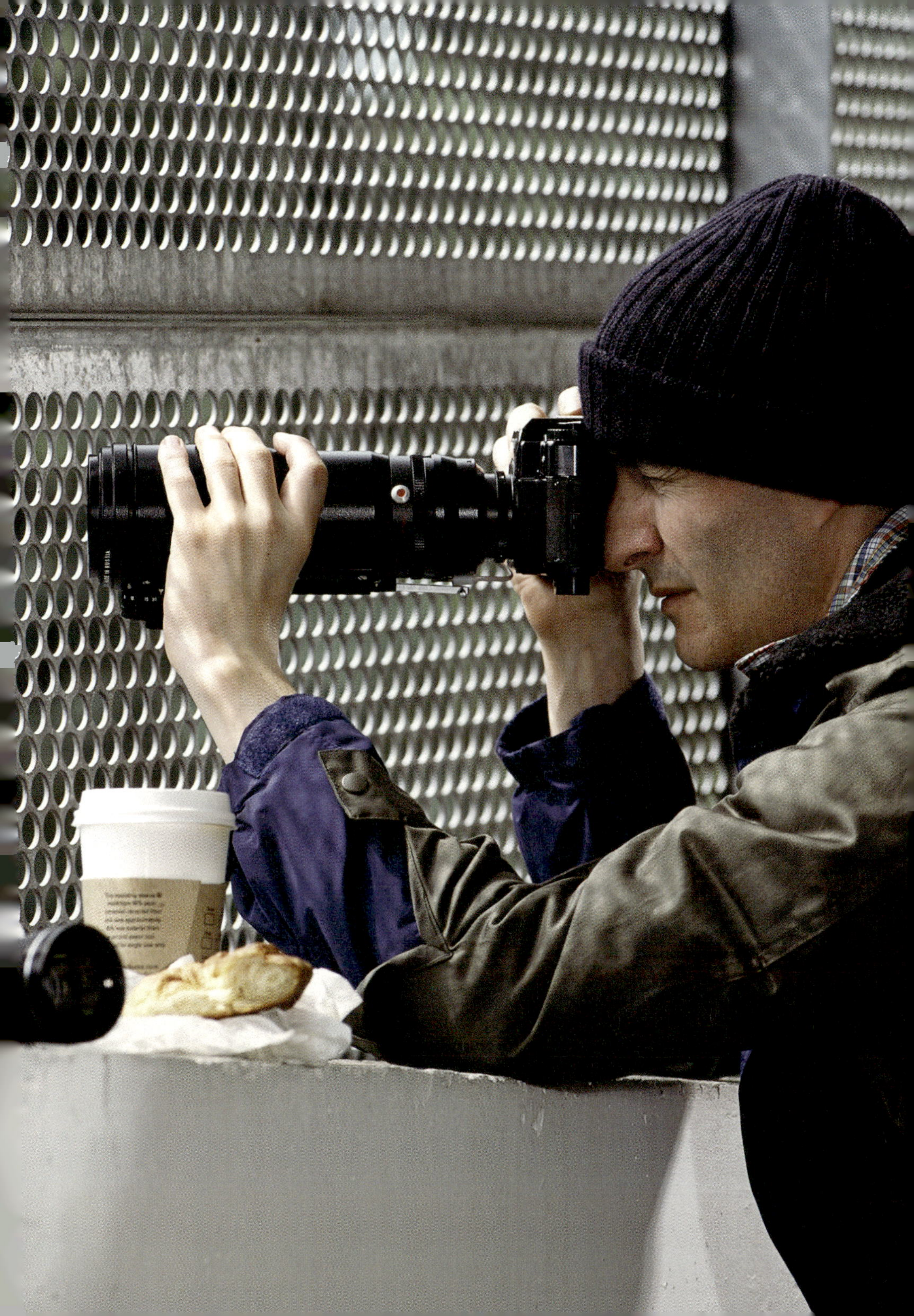

誰のために仕事しているかを忘れない

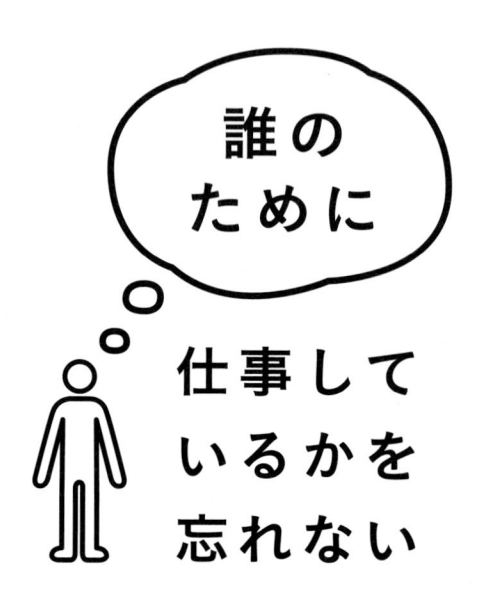

Don't forget who you're working for

誰のための・何の仕事かが明確なことは、ダイレクトでシンプルな原動力となる。私が提供できたサービスがその誰かの未来へ、どのように働くかを考えながら仕事をする。

A clear idea of who or what you're working for is a direct and simple source of motivation. Make sure you keep in mind whose future the service you're providing is helping to build, and how it's going to create that impact.

47

先輩のフンでもいい

Shadow people

普段は半歩後ろを歩き先輩を立て、時には一歩前で下準備をこなす。いつも同じ先輩について回ることで、仕事のやり方が覚えられる。自分で考えるよりもずっと早いので、ピタッとくっついていこう。

Walk just behind your superiors to flatter them and make them feel good, but once in a while, stay one step ahead of them to make sure things are ready. You'll remember how to get things done if you keep shadowing the same superior. Cling to them like a leech — it's much faster than trying to work it out yourself.

49

会いたい人に会いに行こう

Go meet the people you've always wanted to

営業を始めたころは右も左もわからず、業界内での地図も持ちあわせておらず、営業する相手への根拠はその仕事を見てみたいということだけだった。そんなお気楽な動機で来られたほうも迷惑だったかもしれないが、見たい、行きたいという欲求は仕事の根源として大切にしたいものである。

When you just got started in this business, you didn't know your left from your right, and had no idea how the industry worked. The only thing you could use to situate or contextualize the person you were working with was the job itself. That sort of innocent, carefree motivation might have been something of a nuisance for all involved, but the desire to see things and go places is something that you should cherish as the basis of your work.

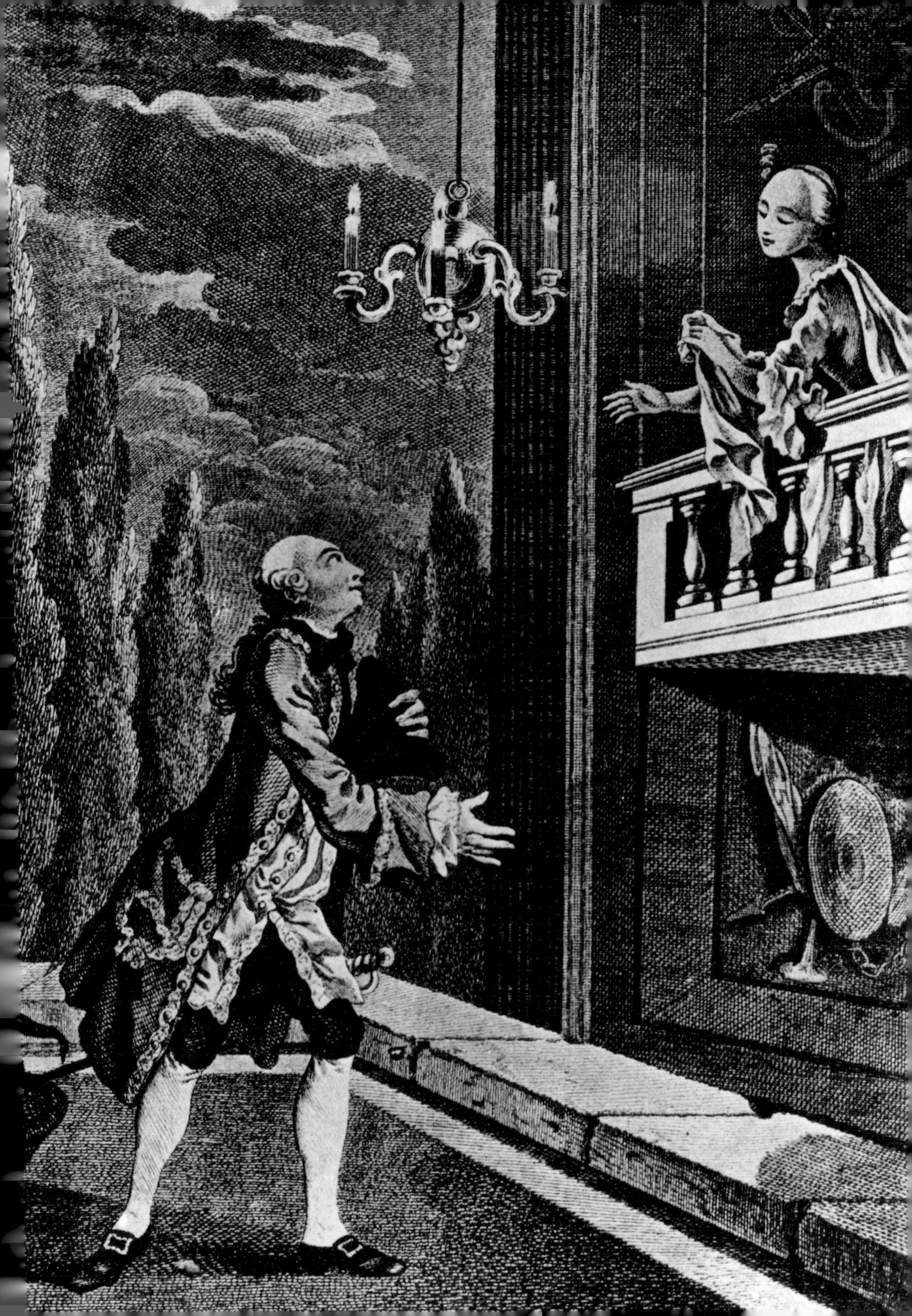

多くの選択肢を提示しよう

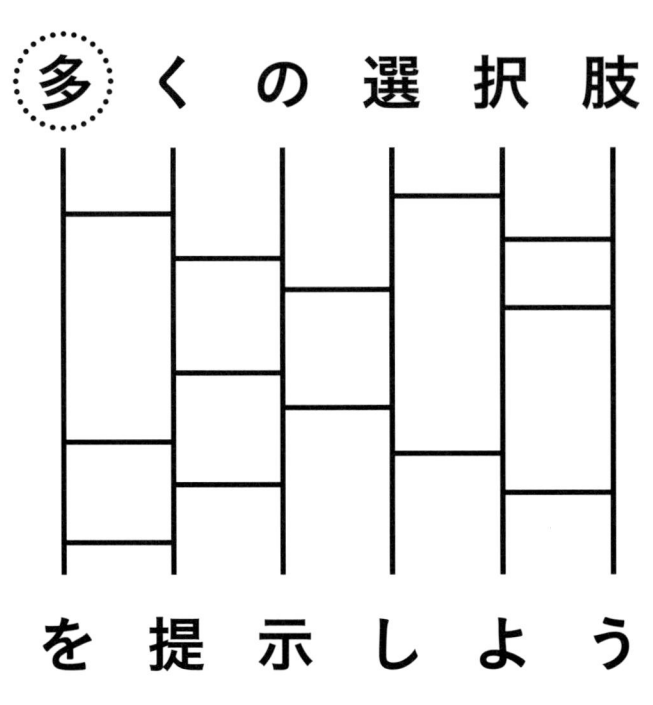

Provide lots of options

仕事相手に比較検討できる材料を提示することや、考えたプロセスを開示することで、仕上がりが独断とならないように注意しよう。例えば写真ではデジタルでの撮影が主な現在、現場での空間と時間が限られていても、多くのアングルを撮影することが可能である。

Be careful that the finished product doesn't become something dogmatic and unilaterally decided on by providing your collaborators with materials that they can weigh against each other, and making clear how your own thinking process developed. Even now, when digital formats have become the norm for photography, you can still shoot from multiple angles even with limited time and space at the given location.

53

何でも質問しよう
WHEN WHERE WHAT WHY WHO HOW

Ask anything

まず自分の取り組むべきデザインへの知識を貯えることが必要だ。右も左も分からないときは、先輩やビジネスパートナー、生産現場の職人などに何でも質問して実地で覚えること。「若いころの恥は恥ではない」とよく言われるが、実際に分からないことを素直に聞ける人は少ない。すぐ質問できることは「才能」である。そうして、時間をかけて身に付けた知識はあなたを裏切らない。

First, you need to store knowledge about the designs you will be working on. If you are confused, ask any question to your predecessors, business partners, or workers at a production site, and learn practically. It's often said, "shame in your youth is not shame", but only a few people can actually be honest and ask about what they don't know. The ability to immediately ask is a "talent". The knowledge acquired through taking the time won't disappoint you.

55

ご機嫌に振る舞おう

Always be in a good mood

優秀な表現者で不機嫌な顔をしている人はいない。デザインの秘密を本当に知っている表現者は、真のコミュニケーターでもある。表現者の苦悩を一身に背負っているような不機嫌な振舞いは、自信のなさの裏返しであることが多い。

I don't know any top creators who go around with a long face all the time. Designers who have a real grasp of the tricks of their trade are real communicators. A sullen face that carries the weight of its troubles on its own shoulders is often just the flip side of a lack of self-confidence.

57

気の小ささをもとう Stay timid

あくまでも対象は人のもの、気の小ささは慎重さとていねいさを生む。気が小さいことは相手にとっていいことである。

We're dealing with people here — being timid helps you to become prudent and discreet, and is beneficial for the other person as well.

59

小さなことからコツコツと

Peck away steadily
at the small stuff

確実にていねいにやることが大事。植えた種は、毎日水やりをする積み重ねで綺麗な花が咲く。そうすると見る人に感動を与え、また見に来たい！　この人に育ててもらいたい！　お願いしたい！　となるはず。

Careful, diligent, and steady work pays off. Beautiful flowers bloom when plants are watered and cared for every single day. People who see your work will be impressed, come back for more, hire you back again, or want to come under your wing.

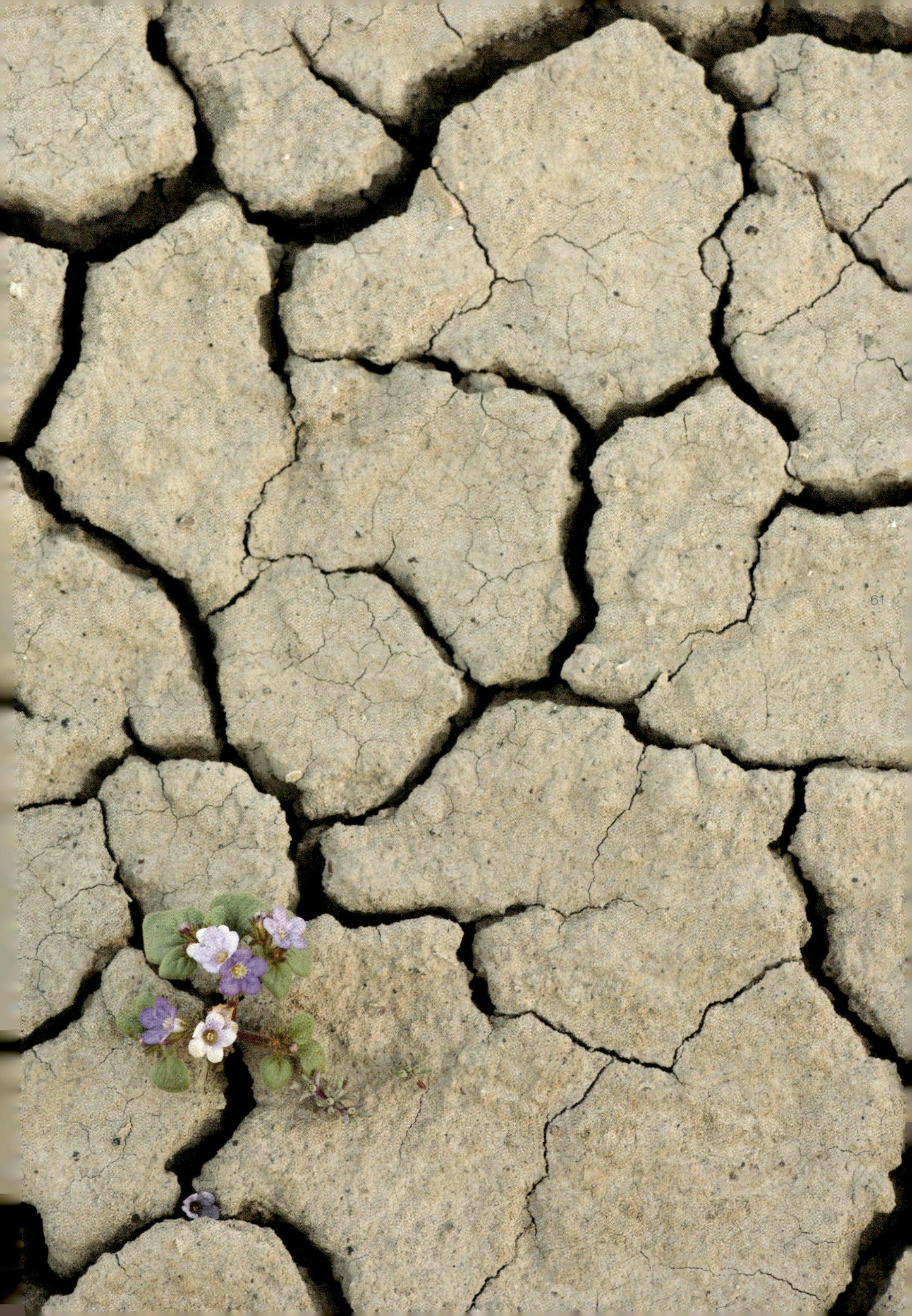

いい空気をつくろう

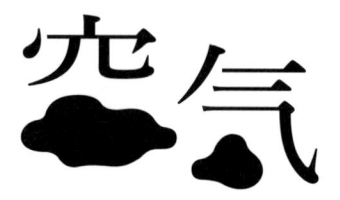

Keep the atmosphere comfortable

現場にいる人によって仕事の結果が影響されることがある。いい影響・悪い影響。こちらから早めにいい空気をつくれるように努める。

The people who are present sometimes influence results — in a good or bad way. Make an effort to create a comfortable atmosphere early on.

63

苦手な人に相談しよう

Sound out people you
don't really click with

行き詰まってしまったとき、自分に似た考えの人や仲のよい先輩に相談すると、想定内の安心した答えが返ってくる。想像の範疇を超えない活動で行き詰まっているのであって、心が落ち着くだけで、たいして解決にならないことが多い。自分の手に負えないのだから、思い切って苦手な人に相談してみよう。真逆で新鮮な意見が聞けるかもしれない。

If you discuss things with people who think like you do, or with superiors that you have a good relationship with when you're stuck, you're going to get answers and advice that you anticipated anyway. You ran up against a wall while engaged in something that didn't exceed the scope of your own imagination, so this approach doesn't usually lead anywhere. This is a problem that's too much to handle by yourself, so take a risk and ask someone that you might not be completely comfortable with. You might actually hear a new perspective on your plight.

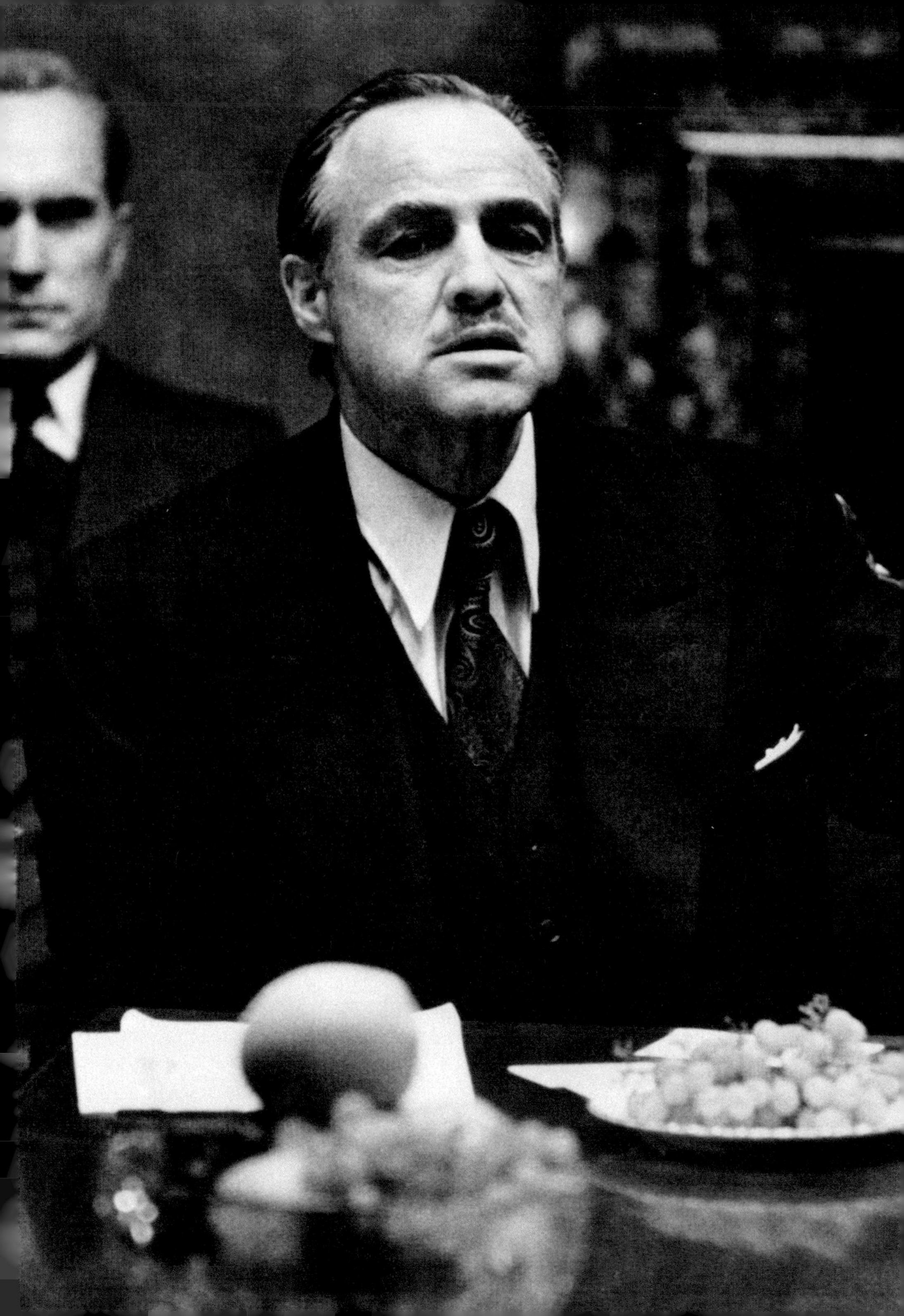

無駄話で要望を聞き出そう

Determine what the client wants through small talk

具体的なかたちがみえていない状況でデザイナーに仕事を依頼することが多々ある。その案件にかけられる時間がない場合もあれば、デザイナー頼みの場合もある。でもその出来映えには文句をいろいろと付けてしまい、なかなか完成形が見えなくなってしまう…これは非常によくあることだが、コミュニケーションを密にすることである程度は防ぐことができる。無駄話のなかで、相手の趣味・嗜好性などを探っていくのである。

Clients often commission work from designers before they have a concrete idea of what they want or need. Sometimes they don't have the time to spend on the project, while other times they just trust the designer to do what's best — before coming back to nitpick and find fault with what you've come up with. This results in a poor idea of what the final product should be. This situation is extremely common, but thorough communication between the two parties can help to prevent it. Try to suss out your client's tastes and preferences by making small talk with him.

67

クリンチ しよう
Clinch

どうにもいかなくなったら、クリンチしちゃおう。綺麗なストレートパンチはなかなか打てないものだ。ジャブ、ジャブ、ガード、ジャブ、ガード。いつも自分のペースとは限らない。

Try clinching if it looks like you aren't going to get anywhere. A clean, straight punch rarely gets the job done. Jab, jab, guard, jab, guard. This doesn't just apply to your own pace.

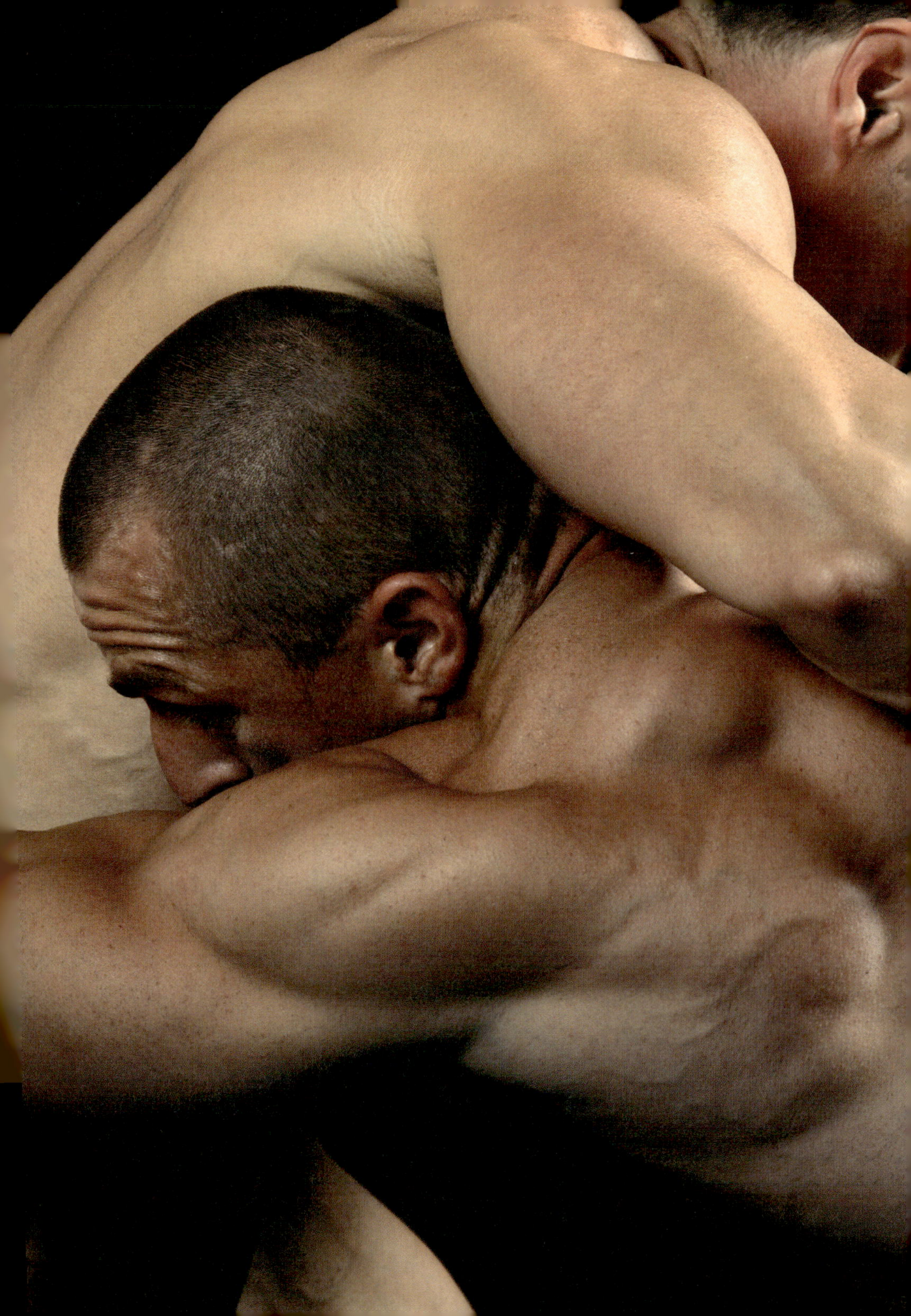

自分の状況を
正しく
把握しよう

Size yourself up accurately

緩やかな下り坂がある事を忘れてはならない。伸び悩み、打つ手をあぐねいている時はその位置に居続けているのではなく、緩やかに下っているのだ。停滞は後退とほぼ同じでその場にいることすら許さない。

There are no flat and even paths you can take when it comes to work. But are you going to notice when the terrain starts to slope downwards ever so slightly? Without realizing that you've quietly started to slide downhill, you find yourself with the mistaken impression that you're still at a point where you're not making any progress. Nope, you're actually starting to regress, my friend. Pay attention if you're slipping, no matter how gentle the gradient might be. You'll be going upwards the next time around.

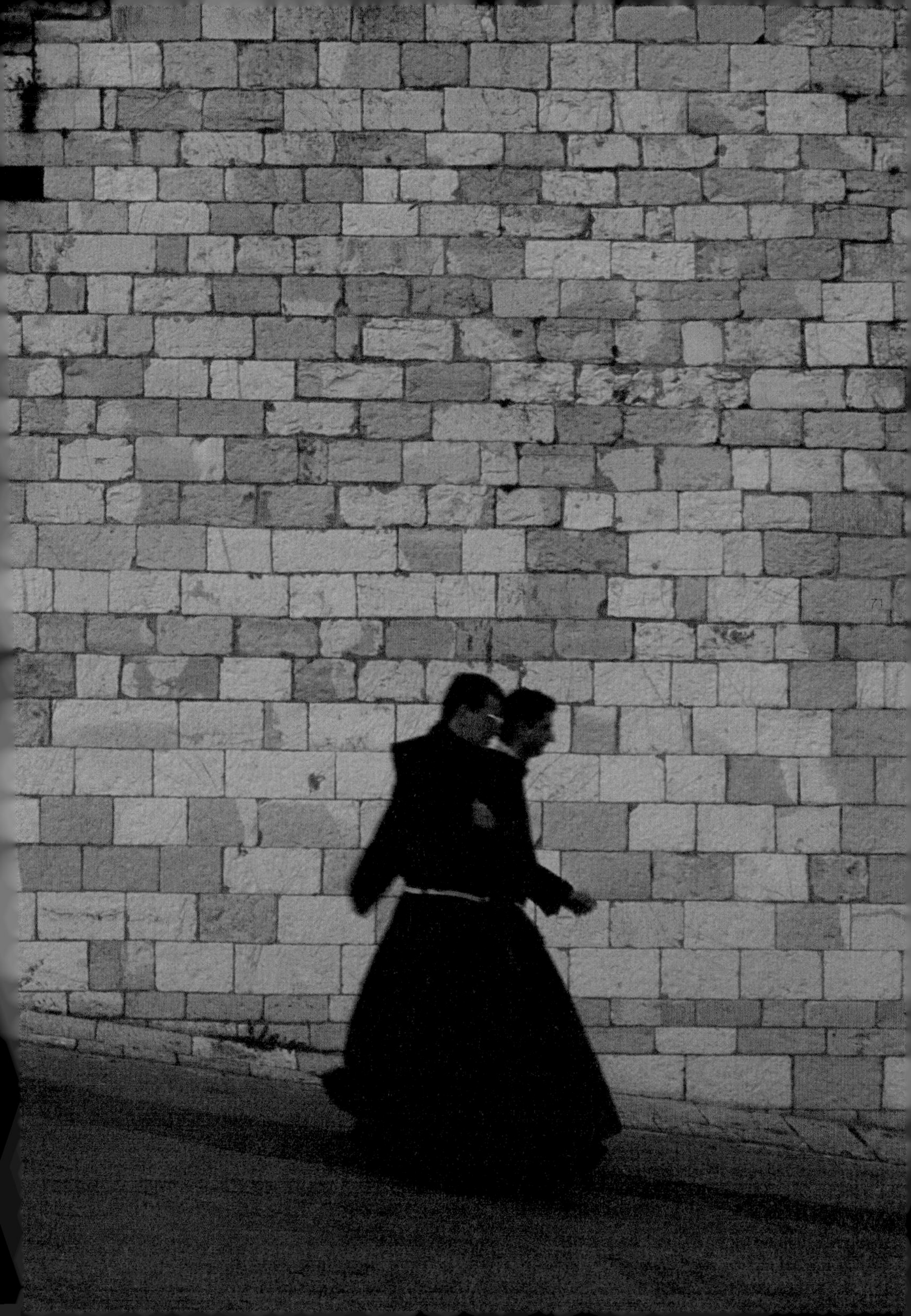

己を知るべし
pile

Know yourself

スポーツにも共通するが、自分の長所、短所を自覚することが大切だ。デザインの場合、特徴がはっきりしないと仕事にならないので、わざとでもいいから長所を尖がらせて出る杭になろう。出る杭は打たれることなくチャンスになる。そして恐れることなく自分ができることを貫けばよい。

Like in sports, it's important to know your strengths and limitations. For designing, work won't be accomplished without clear characteristics; therefore, emphasize your strengths, purposely or not, and be a "stake that sticks out". The stake sticking out won't be beaten but grabs an opportunity. Then, do what you can do, both fearlessly and firmly.

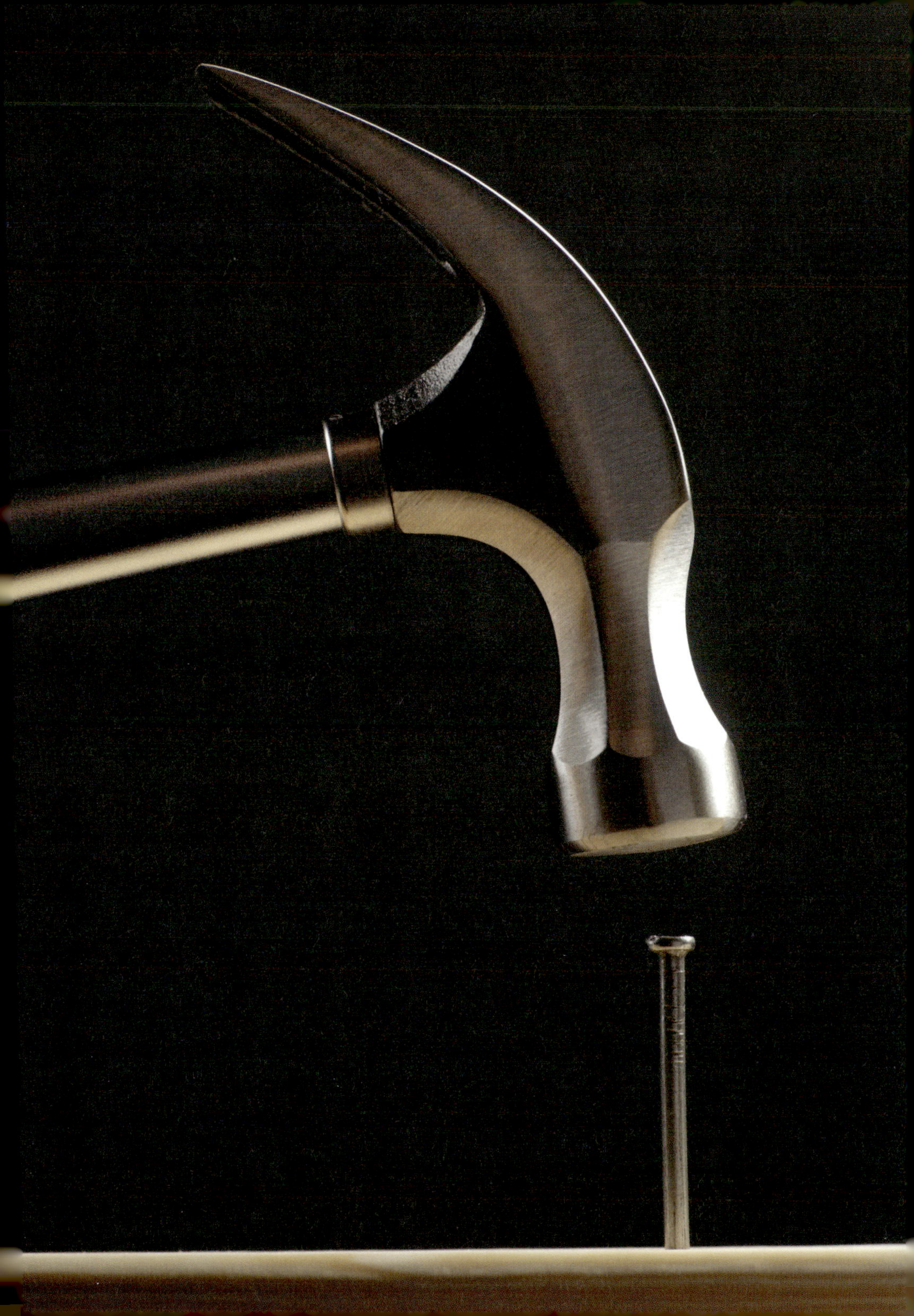

相手が持っている新鮮さを共有しよう

Tap the freshness of your collaborators

こちらは繰り返し行っていることでも、相手には新鮮なことの連続。このことを忘れず、横断的、連続的な仕事で得られた知識、発見を惜しみなく提供する。同じくその新鮮さを共有することで、また別の発見ができるかもしれない。

Don't forget that your collaborators are always going to have something new and fresh to bring to the table, even if you've done this a thousand times. Bearing this in mind, make sure to generously offer them the knowledge and discoveries that you've acquired over the course of your genre-crossing career. In the same way, you might make some other discoveries by sharing this sense of freshness.

実家から届いた
採れたて新鮮野菜！

今日の晩ご飯で早速食べます♪

いいね！・コメントする・シェア・昨日 13:48 ・ⓘ

👍 TARO YAMADA さんと他41人が「いいね！」と言っています。

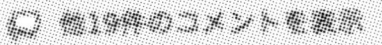

💬 他19件のコメントを表示

田中一郎 おいしそ〜！実家から届くなんてうらやましいよ〜
16時間前・いいね！

Kenichiro Sasaki 新鮮野菜！本当に美味しそうだね♪
晩ご飯も作ったらアップしてね！

リセット
し次へ向かえ

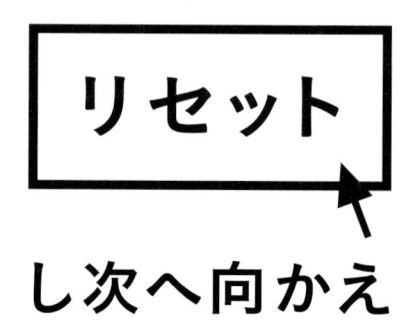

Hit the reset button and
move on to the next thing

クライアントの数だけ異なる種類の仕事がある。それゆえ、1つの仕事が終わり、次なる仕事に向かうときにはこれまでの経験をリセットし、新たな気持ちで向かいたい。成功体験を重ねると我流に陥るケースが多いからだ。いかに素晴らしい経験であっても安易に流用せず、毎回ニュートラルな状態をつくる準備こそがクリエイティブな仕事では大切である。

Every single client you deal with is going to entail a different set of project specifications. If that's the case, you should hit the reset button on all your previous experience when one job ends and you proceed to tackle the next one, approaching it with a fresh mind. The reason is that you tend to become a parody of your own style if you rack up too many successes. In creative fields, what matters is doing the necessary preparation to ensure that you approach each assignment with a neutral stance, without drawing too readily from previous experiences, no matter how amazing they may have been.

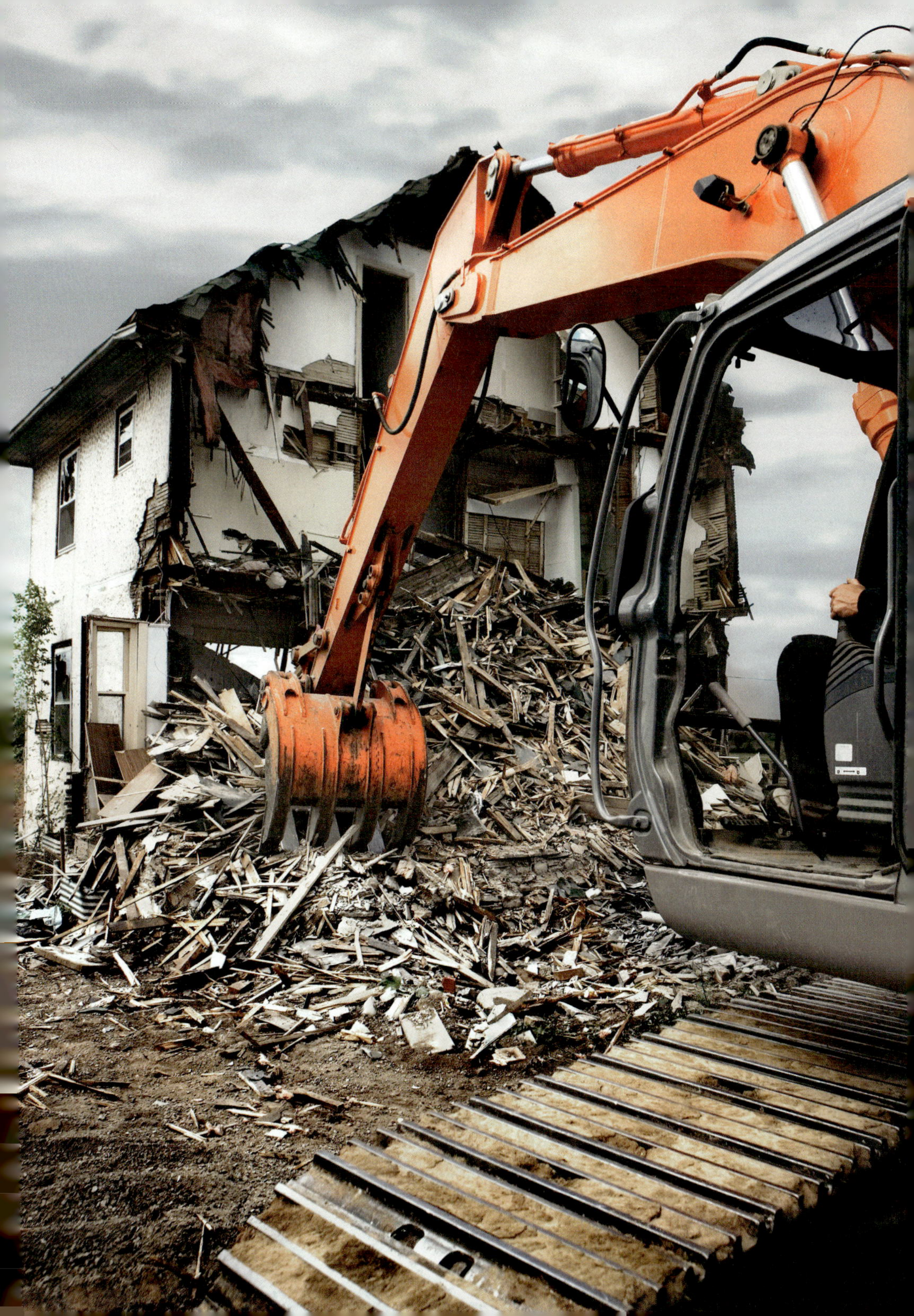

コメントを求められる存在になる

Become someone that people talk about

その分野のエキスパートだと認識されること。「○○といえば、○○さんだよね」という特徴的な部分やポジションを業界内でつくろう。知られていれば、おのずとメディアから声もかかるので、露出は増えていく。

Recognition will come if you're an expert in a particular field. Establish a unique, niche position so that people will automatically associate your name with a specific set of skills or expertise. Once people know about you, media coverage will naturally follow, and your exposure will increase.

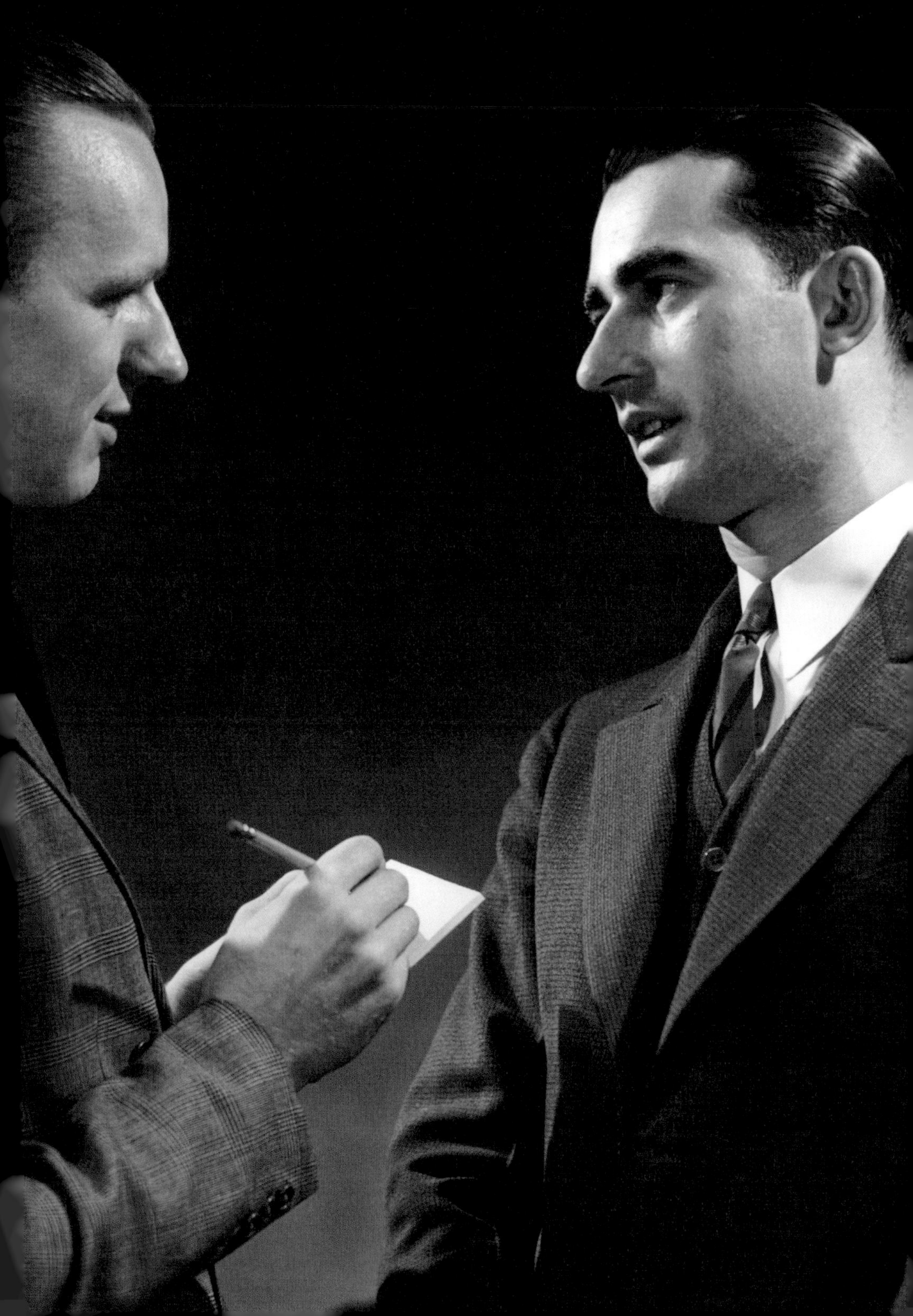

\ No.1 /

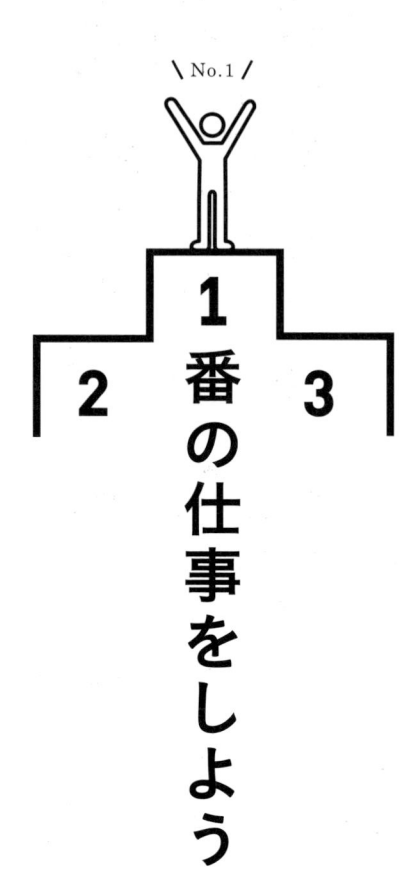

1番の仕事をしよう

Get experience with top players in their own field

どんなに小さな分野でもいい。日本で1番と思える仕事を経験する。「1番がとれる仕事」には、共通する何かが存在する。どんなに小さな分野でも、1度その空気を存分に吸っておくと、すべての仕事に応用できる基準となって体に染み付く。

It doesn't matter how small the field may be. Try doing a job at a place that ranks among the top in all of Japan. There's bound to be something there – a job where only the best people are – that overlaps with your own work. Once you get a good taste of the vibe of that place, no matter how small the field might be, that experience will become a kind of benchmark that you can apply to all of your own projects, and stay with you forever.

81

若さと体力を活かそう

Make full use of youth and stamina

若いからまだまだ時間がある、なんてとんでもない。若いうちしか誰も手取り足取り教えてくれないし、後輩が増えてきたら教える立場が回ってくる。体力があるということは、学べることがたくさんあるということと同義だ。体力を使い切るまで毎日必死に頑張ろう。今が一番頑張れる時期なんだ。

There is plenty of time when you are young--this is a ridiculous lie. You are only attentively taught when you're young, and when you have younger designers you are placed in a position to teach. Having stamina means having plenty to learn. Keep trying hard every day until all of your stamina is gone. Now is the best time to try hard.

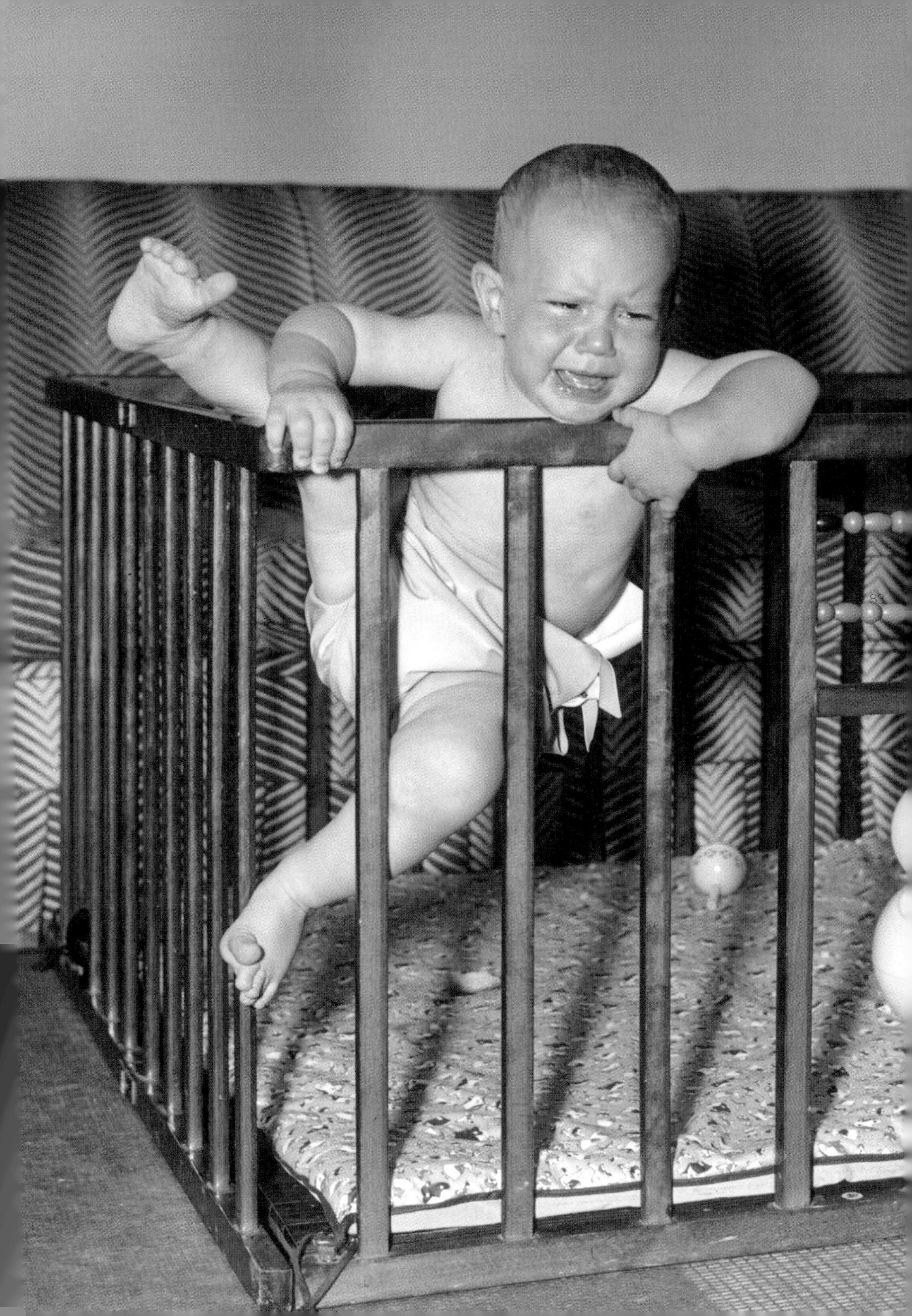

情熱と理想 両輪を回そう

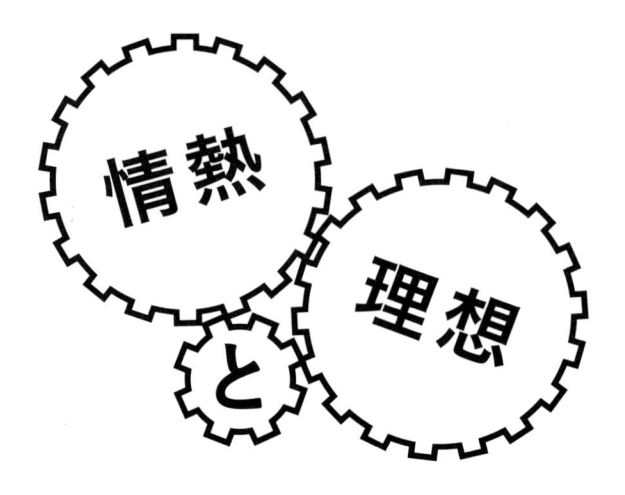

Make both passion and theory work for you

理論のない情熱だけでは、始まらない。情熱のない理論だけでは、伝わらない。何よりも情熱は大切なものだが、情熱だけでは、他人を巻き込む仕事にしていくことはできない。一方、理論だけが先行し、情熱が失われた仕事も他人を動かす力を失っていく。

Pure passion without theory isn't going to get you anywhere. Pure theory without passion isn't going to get your message across. Passion is more important than anything else, but you won't be able to get to do jobs that involve other people. Projects that only emphasize theory but are drained of passion, on the other hand, are not going to be able to move people into action.

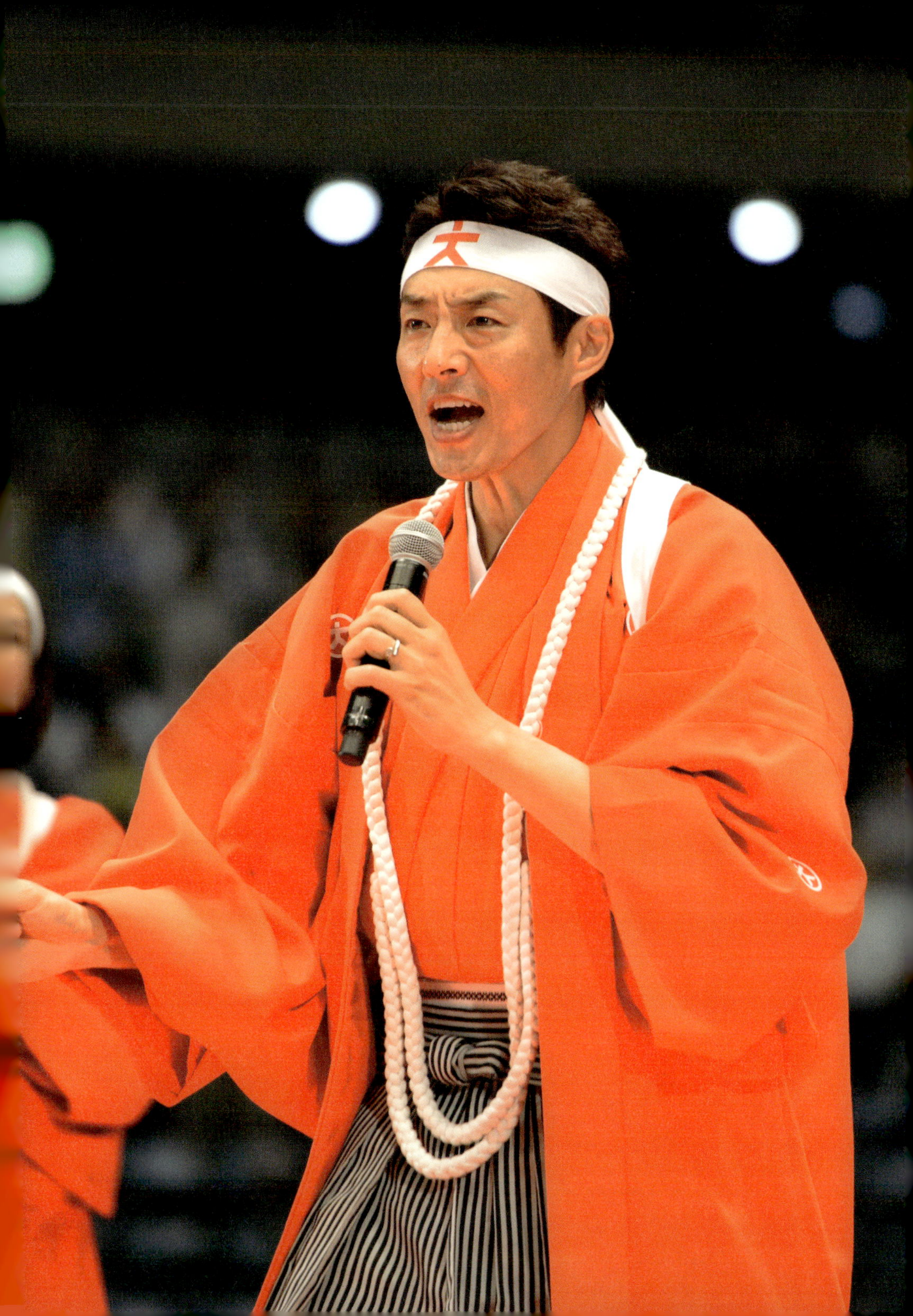
大

「バクリ」ではなく「オマージュ」を

Don't rip off others, pay them a tribute

デザイナーはとかく、人とは違うこと、世のなかにないものをつくり出そうする。そうなると本末転倒、クライアントが求めている成果を出すことが目的なのに、新しいものをつくり出すことが目的になってしまう。よいものはよい。結果、似てしまっても、きっとそれは尊敬であり、敬意の現れ。人はマネをしながら育っていくのである。

What makes designers different from other people is how they try to create things that don't already exist. So sometimes we tend to put the cart before the horse, thinking that the objective is to create something new, when what we should be doing is delivering the result that the client wants. The quality of a good product is self-evident. Even if a certain product ends up resembling something else, there's no doubt that it was conceived with the utmost respect for the original. People learn and develop by imitating others.

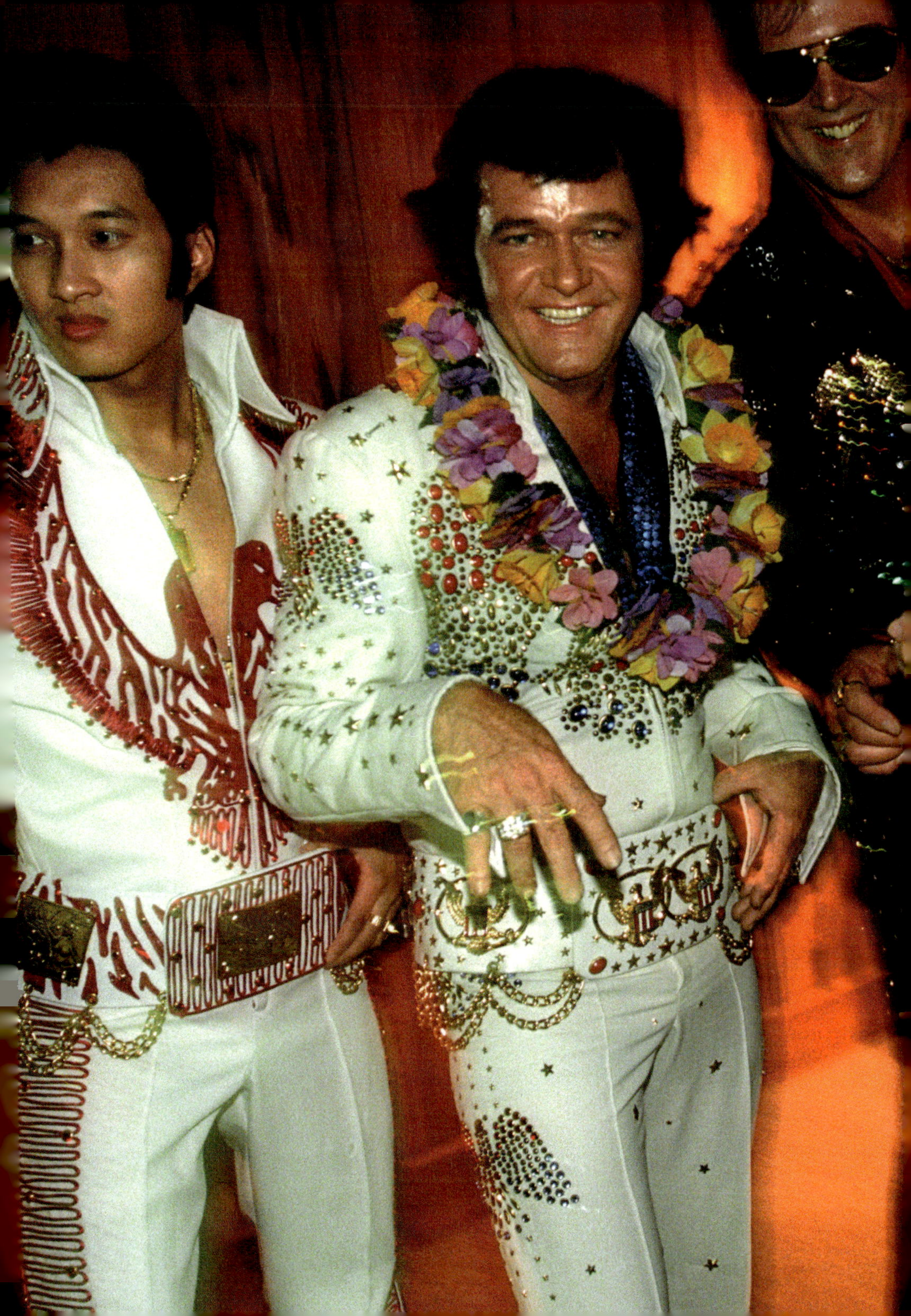

真似るならコンセプトを真似よ

When you copy,
copy concepts

ほかのデザイナーが残した優れた仕事から、見た目や形をまねてはいけない。オリジナルを超えることはできないからだ。しかし、そのデザインの背景にあるコンセプトを真似るのは有効だ。コンセプトを理解し、そこから考え方を学ぶことができれば、自分のオリジナリティを乗せて、別の新しい表現を示すことができるようになる。

Do not copy appearances or shapes from other designers' fine works. It's impossible to exceed the original work. However, copying the concept that lies behind the design is effective. By understanding its concept and learning the designer's way of thinking from it, you will be able to add your originality and present a new expression.

89

できない ことは ー→ 📷 アウト
ー→ ✏ ソーシング
ー→ 📄 しよう

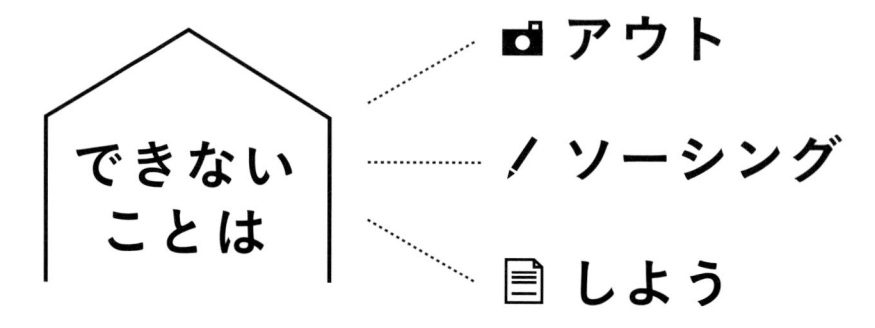

Outsource things that
you can't do yourself

少人数体制で会社を運営するときは、すべてのことをインハウスで行うことは叶わないかもしれない。慣れないことをスタッフにさせるよりも、いつも頼れるプロフェッショナルチームを外部にもっていることで、よりスピーディーに完成度の高い仕事ができる。

You won't be able do everything in-house if you're running a compact firm with a small team on staff. Rather than making your staff handle tasks that they're unfamiliar with, being able to draw on the resources of a professional team outside your firm will enable you to deliver high-quality work at short notice.

チャッ

ファン を増やそう

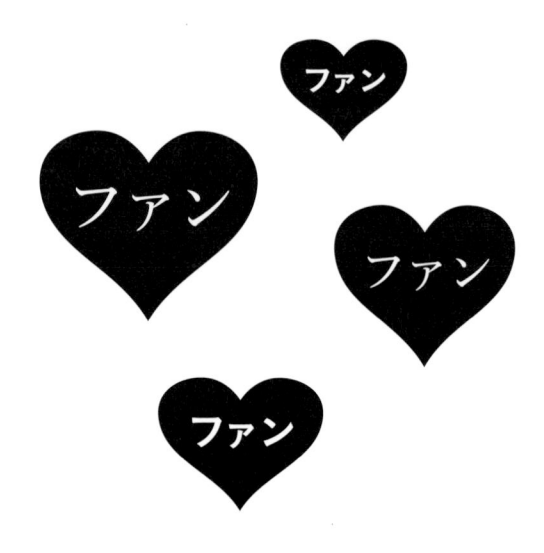

Increase your fan base

最近は「僕は、あんなことやこんなこともできるんです！」よりも「あの人、あんなことやこんなこともできるらしい」のほうが信憑性がある。確かにあなたの評価は、あなた自身ではなく他人がするもの。ということで、あなたのことを勝手にPRしてくれるファンをたくさんつくろう。もちろん、あなたを売り込んでくれる人のPRも忘れずに。

Self-advertising your manifold talents and skills has now become less credible than other people spreading the word around on your behalf. Your reputation is not self-made – it's based on how others evaluate your work. This means that you should try to build a wide fan base that will automatically do your PR for you. Of course, don't forget to return the favor to these folks.

ROMANCE!

価値を産み出す存在になろう

Hold on to your own sense of value

「影響は受けるものではない。与えるものである」というのは、アーティストの森村泰昌による言葉。「何でもあり」は結局「何にもなし」。すべての価値がフラットになり、何をやっても許される状況のなかで、何を「あえて」提示していくのか。世のなかに価値を問う者に求められている課題である。新しい価値を生み出していくためには、ある時点で大きな意識の転換が必要だ。

The artist Yasumasa Morimura once said that "influence is not something you are subject to, but rather something you exert." If anything goes, then nothing has any impact or significance. In a world where all values have become flat and anything is permitted, what are you going to "risk" choosing? That's the task demanded of those who've taken it upon themselves to question the values of this world. In order to create new values, you're going to need a major shift in consciousness at some point.

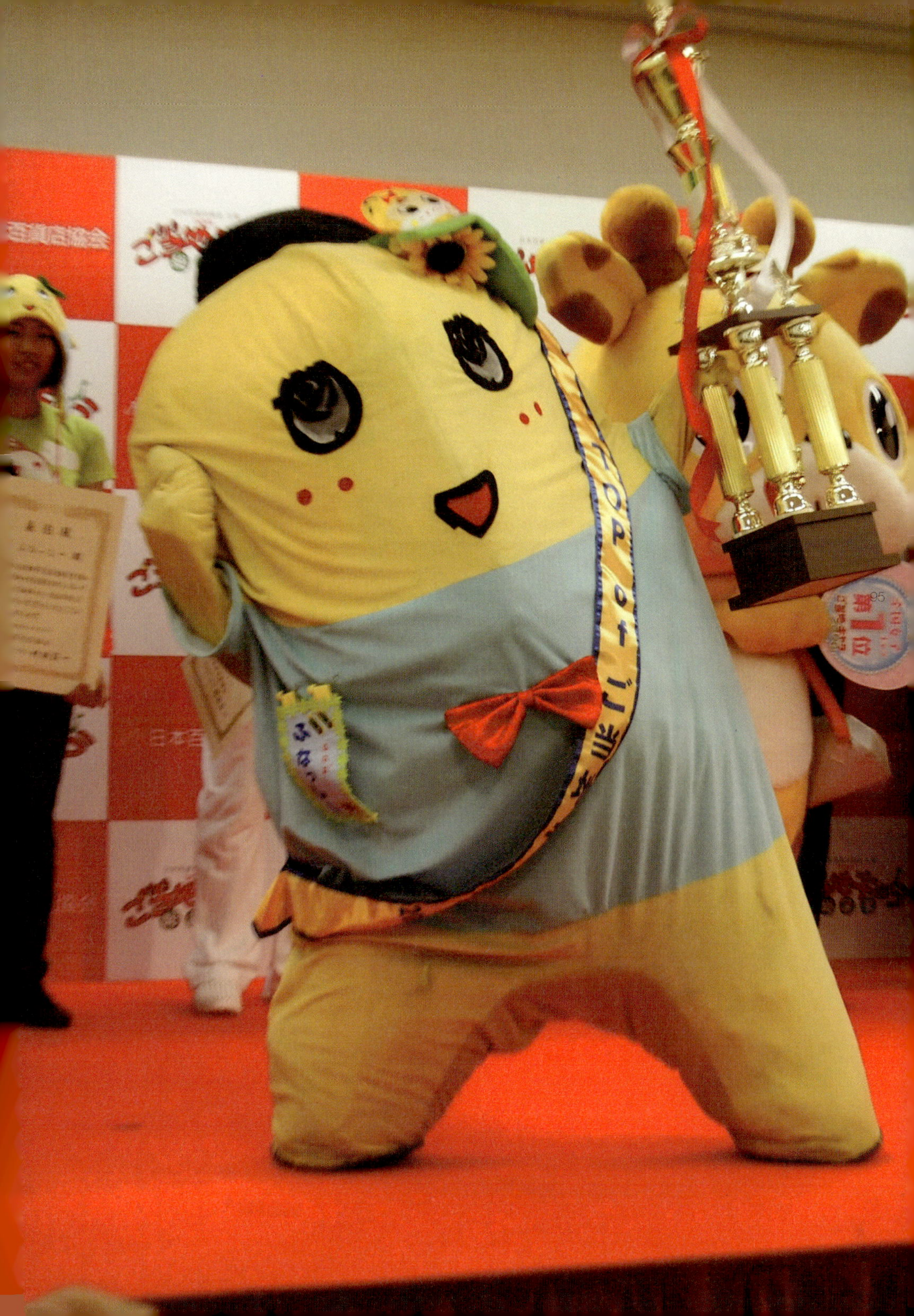
第1位

脳髄
にイメージを建築せよ

Construct an image in the
mind of the viewer

よいプレゼンは相手の脳髄に瞬時にイメージを建築し、くっきりと残像を残す。言葉や絵を駆使して、相手の脳のなかにイメージやアイデアを鮮明に描き出すことができる。その解像度が高まれば共感（シンパシー）が生まれ、信頼関係は強固になる。反対に身内にすら共感されないものは、他者の脳には決して建築されず、世に出すべきではないだろう。誰かの脳に残像が残れば、デザインの第1フェーズとしては成功である。

A good presentation creates momentary images in the mind of the viewer, leaving a clear and sharp imprint. You can trace images and ideas vividly in the mind of the other person using words and pictures. The higher the resolution of those images, the more sympathy you'll be able to elicit, and the more solid your relationship will become. Conversely, things that can't even strike a chord with your own staff are obviously not going to resonate with other people — not at all the sort of work you'd unleash on the world, is it? If you manage to leave an imprint on someone's mind, you've nailed the first step of the design process.

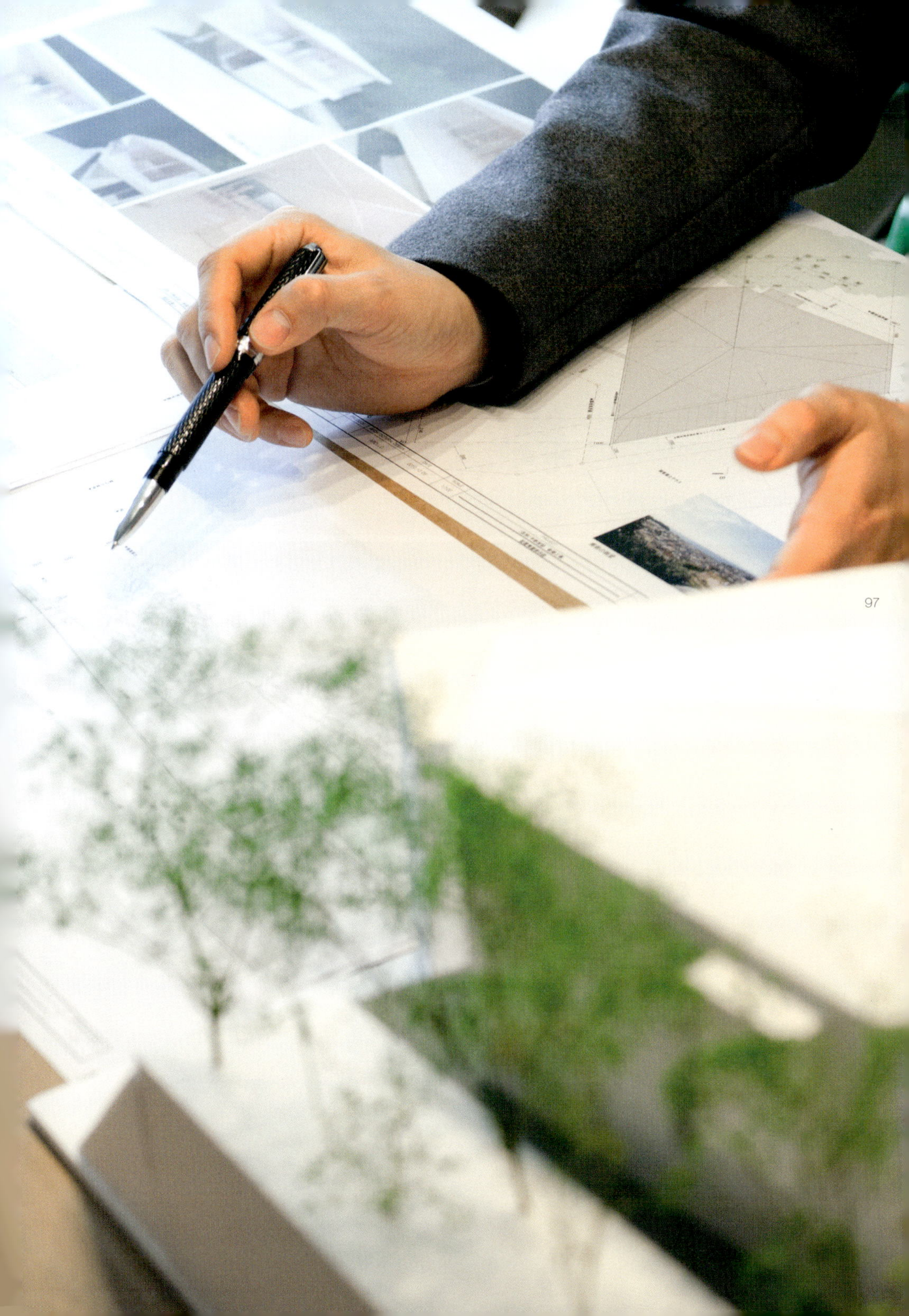

仕事は上手に終わらせよう
Wrap up the job with flair

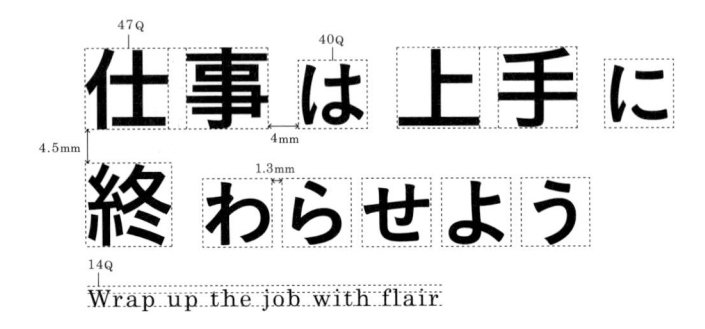

仕事の最後にはクライアントとともに、これまでのデザインプロセスを振り返る機会をつくる。そうすることでデザインは真の完成へと向かう。デザインへの愛着をもち続けてもらう工夫こそがデザイナーの最後の仕事であり、最大の仕事だ。そして、現場にデザイナーの痕跡を必要以上に残さないことも大切である。上手に終わらせて次に向かおう。

At the very last stage of a project, create opportunities to look back on the design process together with your client. This takes the design to its real conclusion. The designer's final — and most daunting — task is to make sure the client takes the effort to continue to develop an emotional attachment to the design. It's also important to ensure that the designer doesn't leave his or her mark on the site.

99

自分の時間に高い価値を付けよう

Set a high value for your own time

ヒット商品が出れば青天井に稼げる商売と違って、請負のデザイン業は自分の時間だけが資源だ。自分が切り売りできる時間が尽きれば、それ以上仕事は受けられない。また同じ仕事は二度とないから、毎回新しいデザインに取り組まなければならない非効率的な仕事だ。自分の時間に高い価値を付けるためには、短時間で高い価値の付くデザインを用意するしかない。その一点に集中せよ。

Unlike businesses that create limitless revenue when something makes a big hit, your time is the only resource for the design contract work. You cannot accept an offer when your available time is exceeded. Furthermore, since the same work is never offered twice, designing is an inefficient process because you must create a new design every time. The only way to set a high price for your time is to create a design with high value in a short amount of time. Concentrate on that.

高収入
アルバイト

初心者・未経験者大歓迎!!

フリーターさんやOLさんにオススメ!

短時間でガッツリ稼げる!

日6,000円

SHONEN ○○○○○○!!

自身の言葉をもとう

Hone a language that is your own

自分の考えていることを他者に理解してもらうために、いかなるポイントでどのような言葉を使えばよいかという準備を常にしておきたい。ものごとの感覚をつかむ能力のある人は、言葉遣いもデリケートだ。しっかりと話すことができない人によいデザインはできない。そしてデザインのよさを言葉で説明できるように常々、ボキャブラリーを鍛えておこう。それは無形の魅力をさまざまな人々に理解してもらうためのサプライヤー側の努力である。

Always prepare yourself to know in advance which words you're going to use in relation to which point, so that other people can understand how you think. People who are good at reading and latching onto the sensations associated with certain things also have a delicate touch when it comes to language. Good design tends to be beyond the reach of inarticulate people. Work on acquiring a vocabulary that allows you to always explain verbally why something is good. This is the effort that the supplier needs to make, so that as many people as possible understand the intangible appeal of one design compared to another.

103

ボス不在の日をつくろう
Make time for days when the boss isn't around

常にボスから的確な指示があるわけではなく、そうした際には各自が臨機応変に考えなければいけない。指示系統が存在しないときの動きにこそ、組織の真の力量が出る。ときおり、あえてボス不在の状態をつくってみよう。普段からミドルマネジメント職を仮のボスポジションに置き、トップマネジメントとしての力量を試すことが重要である。

There are not precise instructions from a boss, and each person must always think for adaptation to circumstances in such case. The true ability of the organization is reflected on movement when instructions system does not exist. I will occasionally make a state of the boss absence daringly. I put middle management in the temporary boss position, and it is important that I try an ability.

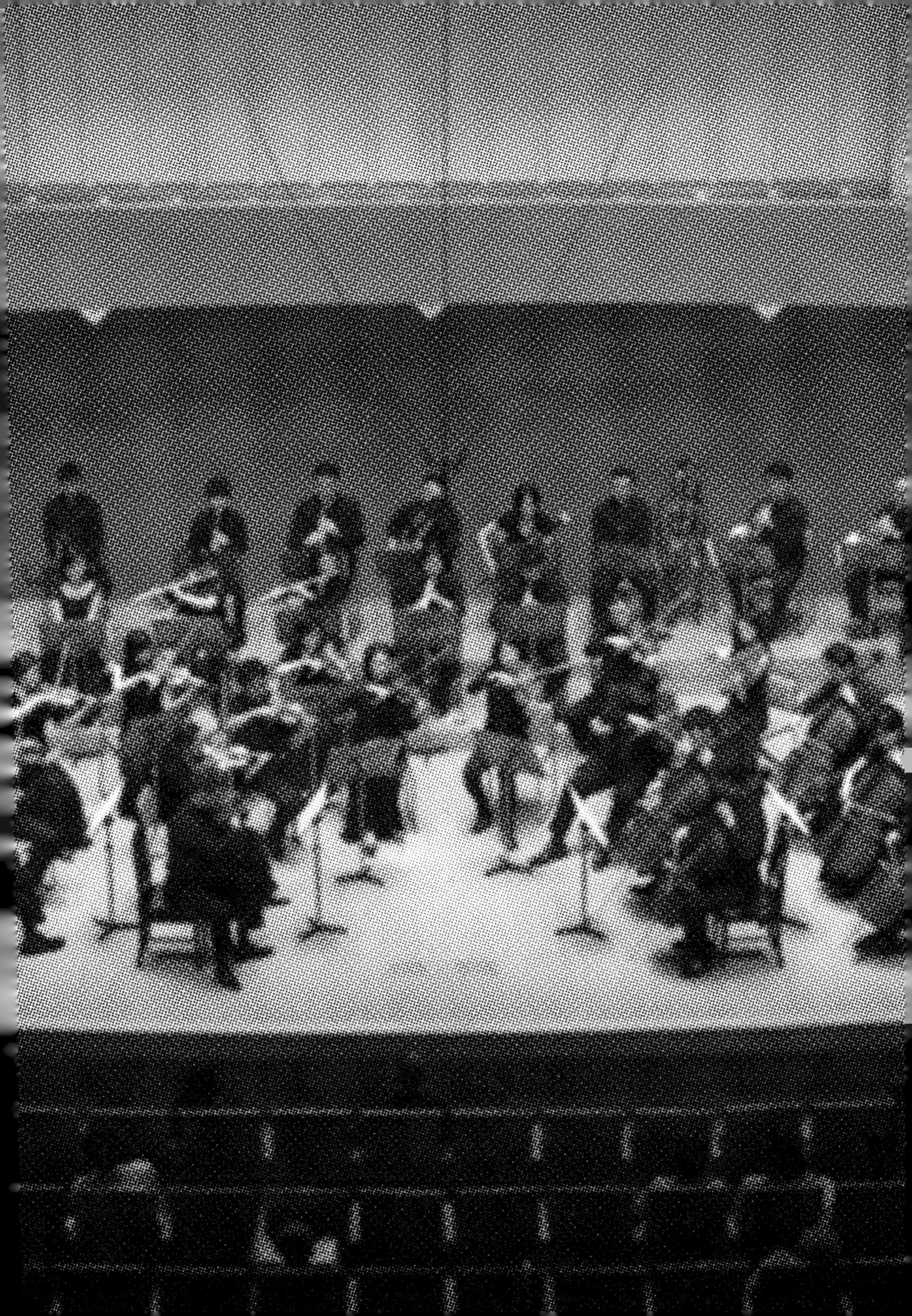

残像のなかに
小さな黒い点を見つけよう
Look for the little black dots in the afterimage

工場のおばさんは顔も動かさずじっと見ている。ベルトコンベアにのってくる車のエンブレムは大群の列をなして、ものすごいスピードで彼女の前を素通りする。彼女は、エンブレムに付いてしまった傷や汚れを発見し、パッと抜き取るという不良品の検品をしているのである。彼女は1枚1枚を見ているのではなく、残像の小さな異物を見極める。同じことを繰り返すと小さな問題点がよく見えるようになるのだ。いつもと違う気がする!? これ大事。

The lady who works in the factory looks straight ahead without moving her face one bit. The endless rows of car emblems on the conveyor belt whiz past her at an incredible speed. It's her job to find defective emblems with scratches or stains on them, and pull them from the belt right away. But she doesn't do the job by looking at the emblems one by one — what she's really doing is staring past them, at the little irregularities in the afterimage of all those objects. By doing this repeatedly, she becomes able to detect all the small problems. Different from the usual — this is important.

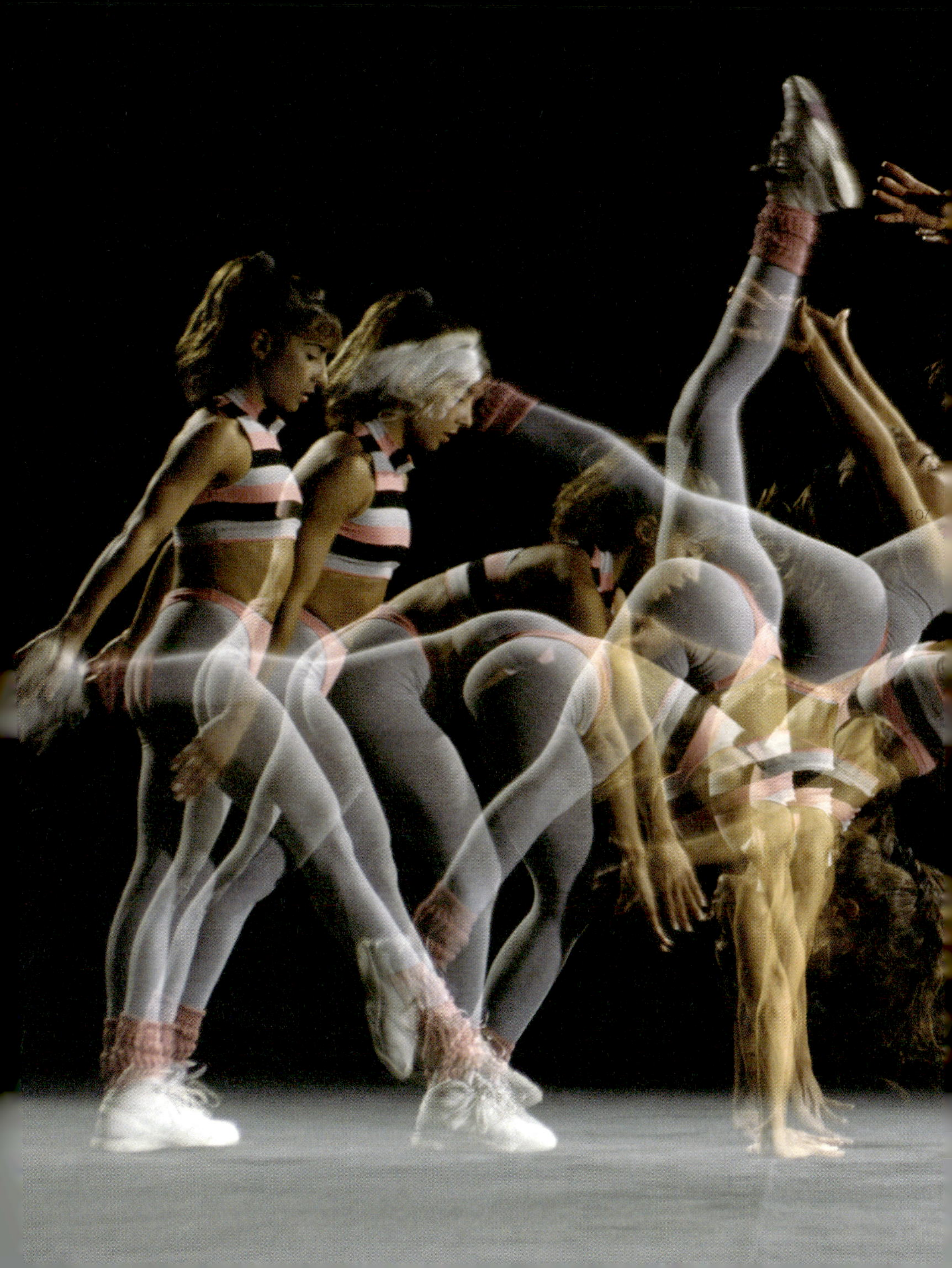

完全崩壊
しなければいい

We're fine as long as we don't completely collapse

デザインやモノづくりを行う会社は夜遅くまで働いていることが多く、徹夜もしばしば。夢と希望を胸に入社したものの現実の厳しさに耐えられず、辞めていく人が多いのもこの分野の特徴。もっとよい会社になるために労働環境をよくすることも1つの方法であるが、求人が多いのもこの分野ならでは。いっそ「辞める人がいても組織として崩壊しなければよい」くらいの心持ちのほうがよいかもしれない。

Design and manufacturing companies tend to have a culture of working late into the night, with frequent all-nighters. Another thing that's unique about this field: the many youngsters who join design firms filled with hopes and dreams, only to quit after realizing that they can't deal with the harsh reality of the industry. One way to deal with this problem is to improve working conditions in order to become a better company, but the constant search for staff is another thing that's particular about the design field. Perhaps a better attitude to have is "even if people quit. we're OK as long as we don't fall apart as an organization."

109

シンプルを極めよう

Refine simple things

「シンプル＝簡単でローコスト」ではない。むしろその逆であり、熟考が必要になる。シンプルを極めるということは、そのなかに含まれるあらゆる複雑性を整理し、序列を付け、無駄を省き、自らの存在をも消していくための極限の努力が必要になる。おびただしい数の検討プロセスのみがデザイン価値となり、その繰り返しによりブランドが生まれる。そのためには時間やお金など圧倒的な自己投資も必要だ。

"Simple" doesn't mean easy and low-cost — the opposite, rather. Simple things require you to mull over them. The act of refining simple things demands an incredible effort to sift through all the complexities that they entail, rank them, eliminate the extraneous — and even a sense of itself as an object. The sole value of design lies in the countless investigative and analytic processes that it involves, and a brand is what emerges from repeated iterations of these processes. That's why design requires an overwhelming self-investment in terms of both time and money.

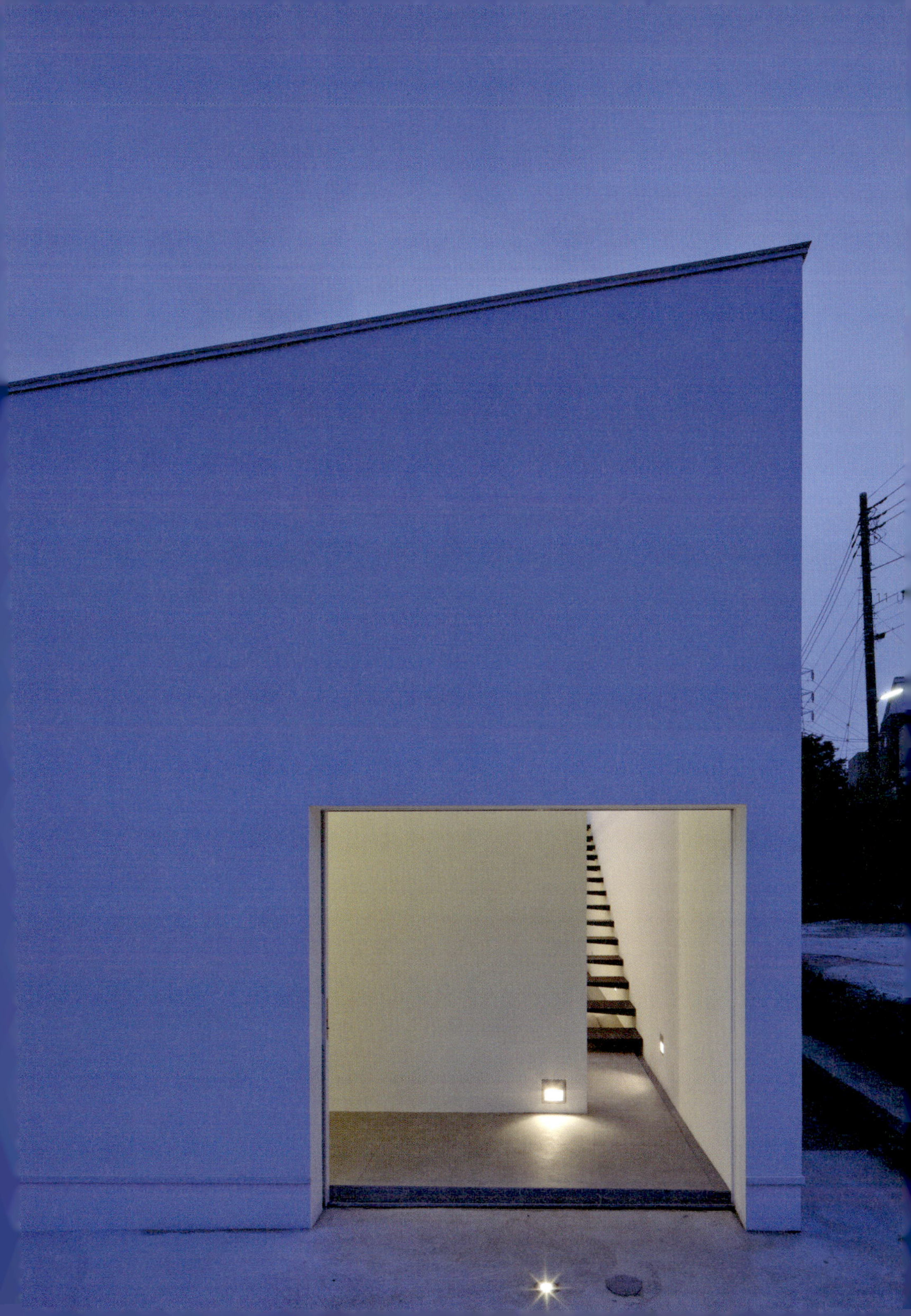

人の
ためになろう

Work with someone in mind

人のためにならない仕事はデザインとは呼べない。よいデザインは人のためになり、その結果として最終的に自分のためになる。自分のためになるということはあくまで結果であり、決して目的であってはならない。これはクライアントに対してはもちろん、デザイナーの卵が上司や師のもとで仕事をアシストする期間にも同様のことがいえる。

Work that doesn't have a particular audience in mind can't be called "design". Good design serves the needs of people, and ultimately becomes something you produce for the sake of yourself. This act of working for yourself is really a kind of end result — it can't be an objective in and of itself. This applies not only to your clients, but also to budding designers who spend a period of time working under their superiors or more senior figures.

Nod うなずこう

日本人の習性、うなずく。相手もバカではない。自分がどう思ってうなずいているのかくらいは伝わっている。でも、いちいち反応してくれていることも伝わり、それは好感触になるはず。意味もなくうなずく相手に不信感をもつ相手はそういない。

Nodding — that most Japanese of habits. The other person is no idiot, you know. He can tell what you're thinking when you nod at him. On the other hand, nodding also tells him that you're reacting to everything he says and does, which ought to give him a good impression of you. There aren't too many people who would distrust someone who nods without good reason.

115

デザインは誰のモノかを見つけよう

Whose design is it?

自分なりにどんなによいデザインができたとしても、そのデザインを使ったり、感じたりしてくれるユーザーにとって手に負えないデザインになってしまっては、意味がない。デザインは誰のモノなのか？ それを見つけることができれば、デザインの50%は完成である。

No matter how great a design you manage to come up with, it's not going to mean anything if the end users who will actually interact with the product are going to find it unwieldy. Who are we designing for? If you can answer that, half the battle is won.

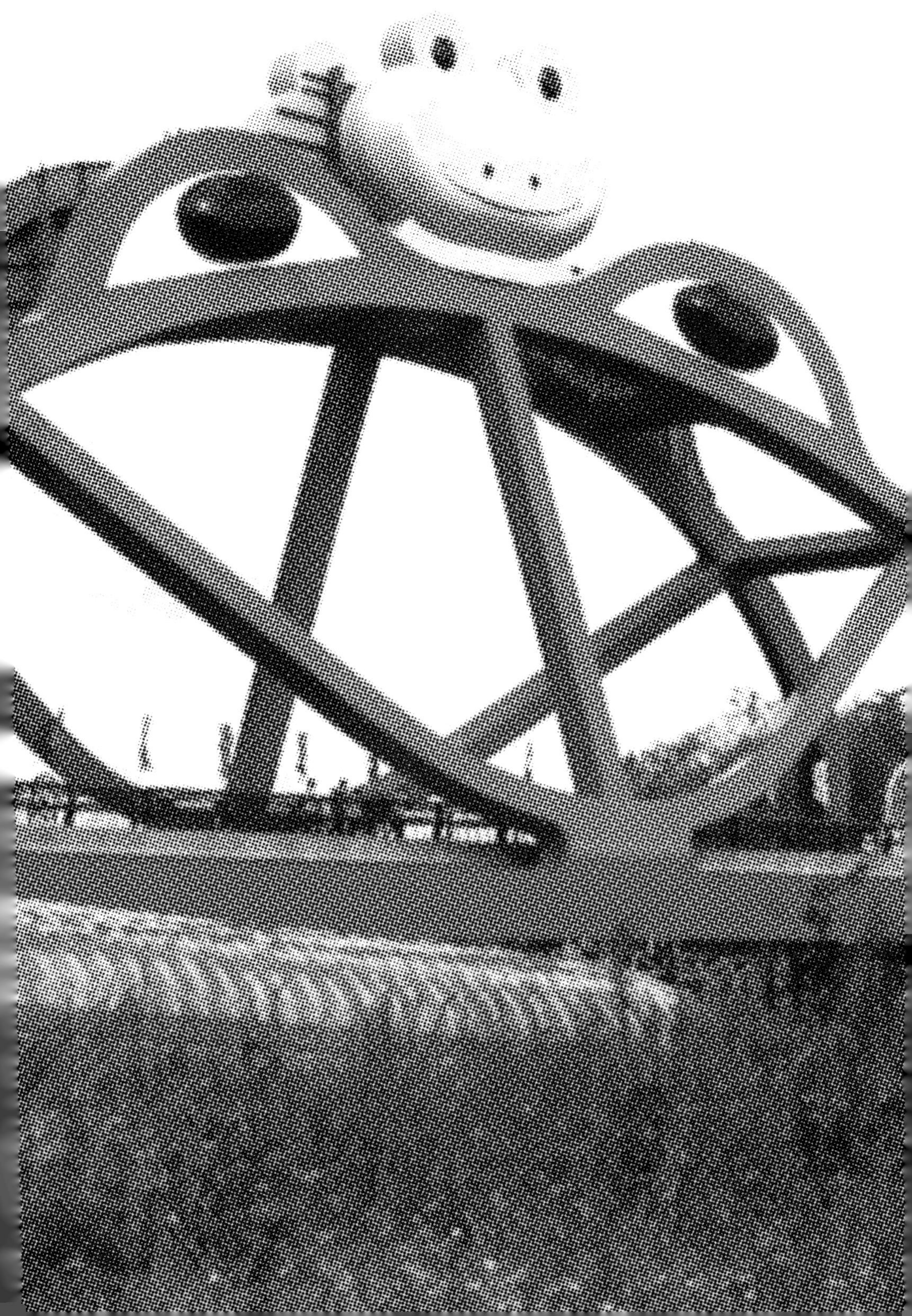

A デザイン
B デザイン
C DESIGN

で他者を満足させよう

Satisfy others with your design

デザインの仕事は他者を満足させて初めて価値を持つ。自己満足のデザインを生み出すのは実は簡単だ。他者の視点に立ち、そのアイデアを批判する作業を行おう。それでも形を変えながらしぶとく這い上がってきたデザインこそ本物だ。そして、デザインを見せるということは、一種のエンターテインメント。ちょっとした打合せでも、大掛かりなプレゼンテーションでも、必ずクライアントの期待や想像を超えるアウトプットを出すこと。

Design work has value only when the designs satisfy other people. It's actually easy to create self-satisfactory designs. Review your idea from the other person's perspective and criticize it. Though they change in form, designs that tenaciously survive this are the genuine ones. In addition, a design presentation is a form of entertainment. Regardless if it's a small meeting or a large-scale presentation, you should always present outputs that exceed the clients' expectations and imagination.

119

良い写真を撮ろう

Take good photos

デザイナーにとって、写真ほどよいマーケティングツールはほかにない。メディアはすてきな写真で誌面を飾りたいし、実物を見られない海外誌のライターはメールに添付した写真から文章を書いたりする。デザインアワードやコンペに応募する際にも写真は大きな役割を果たす。デザイナーのポートレートもしかり。パブリックイメージとして、印象に残るような1枚を用意しておきたい。

Photography is the best marketing tool that a designer can possibly have. Magazines love to have nice photos within their pages, and correspondents for international publications who don't have access to the real thing will write articles based on photos attached to your emails. Photos also play a key role when applying for design awards and submitting work to competitions. Make sure you have a proper portrait taken, too — it's your public image we're talking about, so you'd better have a picture that will make an impression.

No.1 Takahiro

No.52 Hitoshi

泳がせない

Always keep one eye on your staff

部下のやっていることを見逃すこともなければ、泳がすこともない。いちいち怒る。まるで監視しているようだとも言われる。だが実際は1日のうち1人に対して1時間も真剣にみれば限界。ほかの時間は意識の共有すらできていないと思う。せめてもの1時間は真剣に向き合うことにしている。一緒にいる時間まで放任では、ほとんど共有はできない。

Don't let anything your staff do pass you by, but also make sure you don't leave them entirely to their own devices. Get mad at every single thing they do, to the point where they feel like they're under constant surveillance. Keeping a serious eye on one person for one hour in one day, however, should be as far as it goes. The rest of the time, you won't even be able to be conscious of each other's existence. Make sure that you have at least one hour of serious face time. You won't get anywhere if you let even the amount of face time with your staff take its own course.

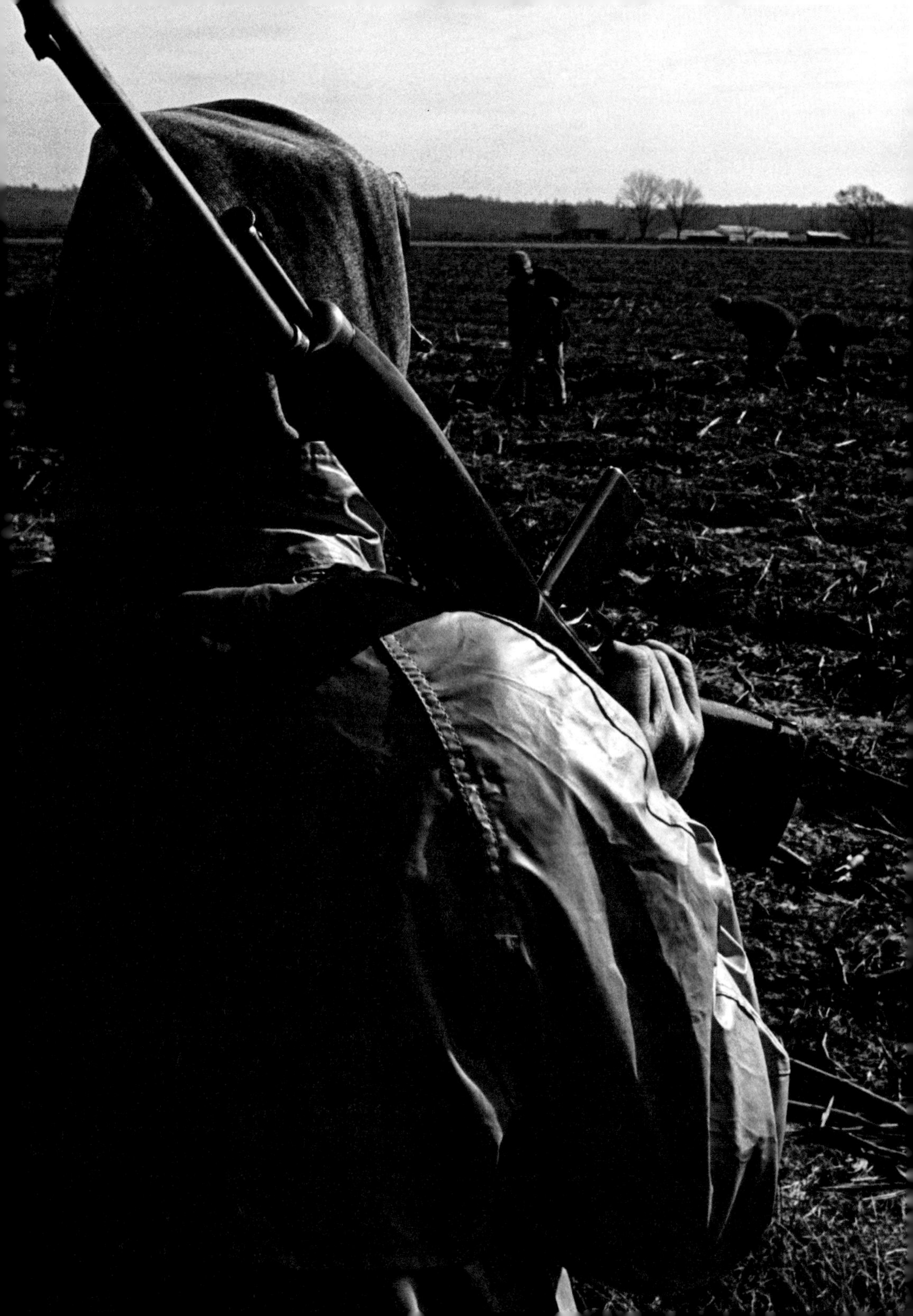

異文化コミュニケーションをしよう

Participate in cross-cultural communication

海外で仕事をするには、意志交換したいというエネルギーがあれば意外と何とかなる。身振り手振り、筆談、なんでも方法はある。相手は優れたデザインがほしいのであって、デザイナーの語学力をテストしたいわけではない。相手が必要なら通訳を用意してくれるだろう。でもやはり、自分の話す言葉で伝わったほうが正確だし気持ちいいものだ。そのモチベーションが生まれさえすれば、コミュニケーションの問題は解消されたようなものだ。

If you have the energy to communicate, working overseas is unexpectedly easy. There are many ways to communicate, such as with gestures or writing. Clients just want splendid designs, and don't care about testing the designer's language skills. If necessary, they will bring an interpreter. However, communicating in your own words is more accurate and is more satisfying. When such motivation arises, communication problems are mostly solved.

125

海外でも仕事をしよう

Design

Work overseas, too

　できることなら1億3,000万人ではなく70億人をターゲットにしながら、ものづくりをしたい。つまり世界をターゲットにするということ。デザインフィールドは無限にあり、文化や哲学の数だけ答えがある。デザインそのものが雄弁に物語るから、言語の違いはさして重要ではない。語学力により不足するコミュニケーションは、情熱と人間力でカバーするのみ。

If it's something that's within your reach, don't just make things that target the 130 million people in Japan, but the 7 billion people around the world as well. The field of design is limitless. There are as many answers and solutions to design issues as there are cultures and ways of thinking in this world. Design can speak eloquently for itself, so differences in language aren't really an issue. Communication that is lacking in linguistic terms can be made up for through passion and talent.

CAFÉ
IL CIPRIANI
Exclusively Organic

COFFEE
HEALTHY LATTE
VEGAN SMOOTHIE
FRESH FRUIT JUICE
PANINI & SALAD
ORGANIC BREAD
DESSERT

日本人としての気負いは持たない

Do not have an
over-eagerness to be Japanese

「郷に入れば郷に従え」というが、デザインの仕事でいえば従わないほうがいい。なぜなら、「日本人デザイナー」としてのあなたを見て、相手は依頼してきているからだ。あなたの得意なデザインを相手が分かるように少しだけ見せ方を変えてあげれば、喜んでくれるはずだ。ただし、日本は意識しなくていい。あなたのデザインには無意識のうちに日本人らしさがあるだろうし、そこからは逃れられないからだ。

Although the expression goes "when in Rome, do as the Romans do", it is better to not follow this dictum in design work, since the client offered you the job because they considered you a "Japanese designer". If you show them a design that you are good at, which has been slightly modified to make it easier for them to understand, they should be happy. Furthermore, don't be conscious of Japan. Your designs are unconsciously Japanese-like, and cannot escape that fact.

129

二重人格であれ

Have a double personality

オタクな自分とオタクでない自分をもつ。専門に傾倒しながらも、専門外の軸を併せもつことで客観性を獲得できる。どちらか一方だけの軸しかないと、仕事ではなく趣味に終わってしまう可能性が高い。

Cultivate both the nerdy and non-nerdy aspects of your personality. Get an objective view on things by having access to references outside your field of expertise, even as you remain committed to your specialty. If you only have one or the other, you run a high risk of remaining a hobbyist, not a professional.

MYSTERY!

DR. JEKYLL & MR. HYDE

「その1文字」が与える印象を考えよう

Think hard about the impact
that single word will make

デザイナーであれば、送付状のフォント1文字が与えるイメージまでにも気を遣うべきかもしれない。日常的に使う封筒や送付状などのステーショナリーからウェブサイトにいたるまで、対外的に使用するすべてが事務所の顔になる。

Designers ought to think hard about the impression that even a single word in a particular font on your cover letter will make on the recipient. Every object bearing your name that goes out into the world — from the envelopes, letterheads and other stationery that you use on a daily basis to your website — is the public face of your company.

neoplus610
STANDARD TRADE.
TRANSISTOR
www.standard-trade.co.jp
shoca

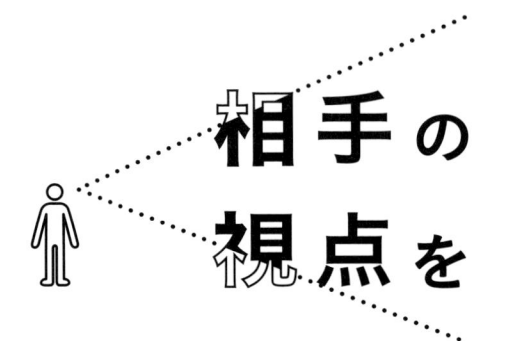

相手の視点を
ヴィジュアルでイメージしてみよう

Visualize things from the other person's perspective

モノや空間が、自分以外の人たちにどのように見えているのか。実際にその視点に立ち確認することで見えてくるものは多い。

How do other people look at objects and spaces? Lots of things become obvious when you actually put yourself in someone else's shoes and verify this for yourself.

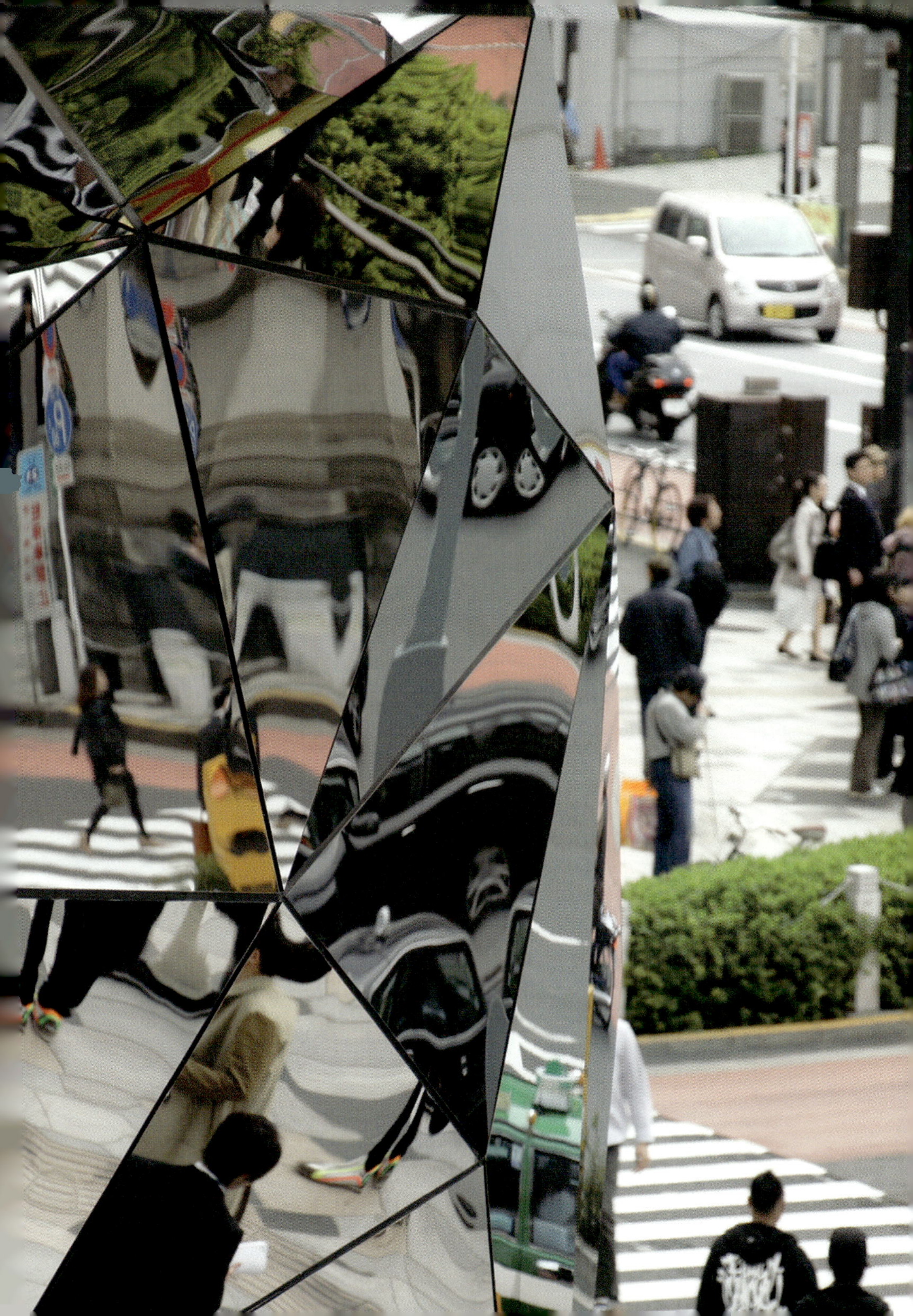

仕事に疲れたら、どうぞ休憩を
Take a break if you're tired

休憩はとっていい。休憩は1つの権利であり、メリハリにもなる。デスクでネットを見ながらお茶を飲むなんて中途半端なことではなく、外に行ってサッカーをやったり、買い物に出たり、一杯飲みに行ったりと自由にしよう。周囲の空気が許さなくとも、ボスはそれくらいのメリハリを許してくれるはず。

It's important to take a break. Time away from work is a right, and it helps to take the edge off a bit. It's not a cop out to have some tea while surfing the Internet at your desk. You should even feel free to go out and play some soccer, do some shopping, or have a drink. Even if it feels like you're slacking off, your boss ought to be fine with that.

137

つくり手とユーザーをつなごう

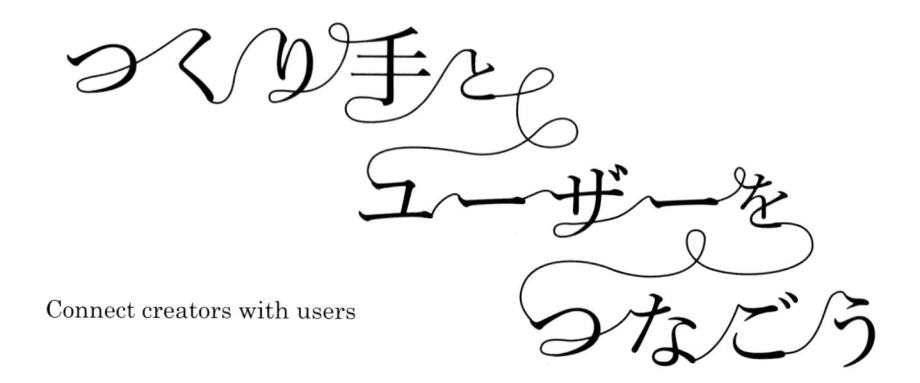

Connect creators with users

モノは最終的には必要としている人のもとにいくが、ユーザーから直接オーダーをもらってつくるものばかりではない。ある程度の量がつくられる製品は、いくつかの中間業者の手を経てユーザーのもとに届くことになる。それは商社だったり店舗だったりするが、その人たちが売りやすいような製品・デザインであることも必要なのである。その人たちがその製品のよさを説明しやすいデザインがあるはずだ。

Products ultimately end up in the hands of the people who require them, but not all of them are made in response to a direct order from the end users. Products that can be manufactured in considerable quantities generally pass through the hands of several middlemen before reaching the user. These middlemen can be trading firms or individual shops, but the products they handle need to sell easily, or have designs that appeal readily to customers. In general, these people are "designed" in a way that allows them to expound on the merits of a particular product.

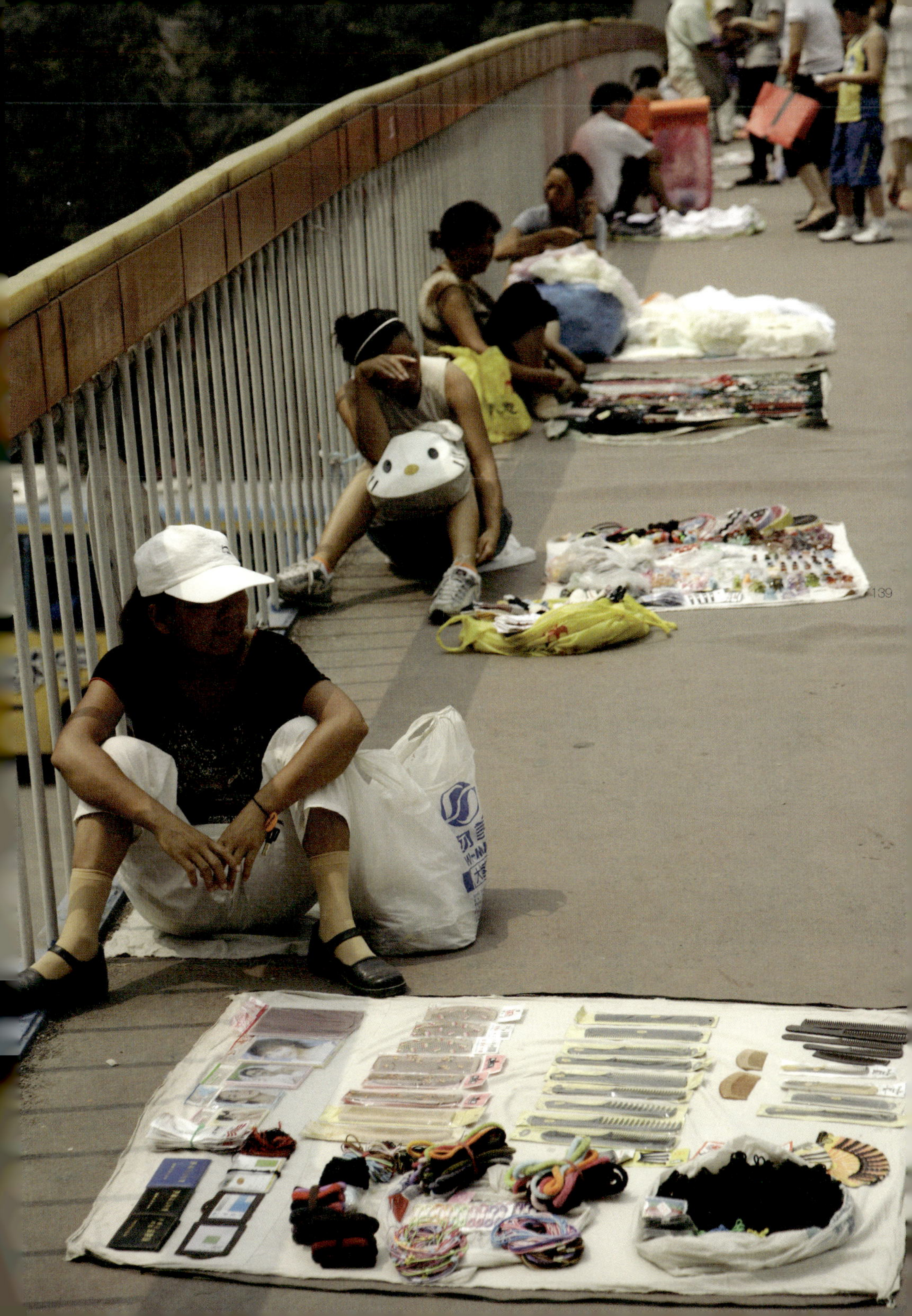

Analyze your own position
and capitalize on it

立ち位置を見極めて生かそう

独立にチャレンジする気持ちはわかるが、トップ下に入ってしまえば独立したも同然。二番手もよい。サッカーの中村俊輔もそうであったように、自分らしくプレーできる場所はトップばかりではない。トップを動かすくらいのポジションもあることを知ってほしい。

It's natural that you want to take on all these challenges by yourself, but the position just behind the striker is also an autonomous one. It's not such a bad thing to stay in the backseat. The frontline isn't the only place where you can make the best of your talents — just like the soccer player Shunsuke Nakamura. The task of supporting the front man is also an important one.

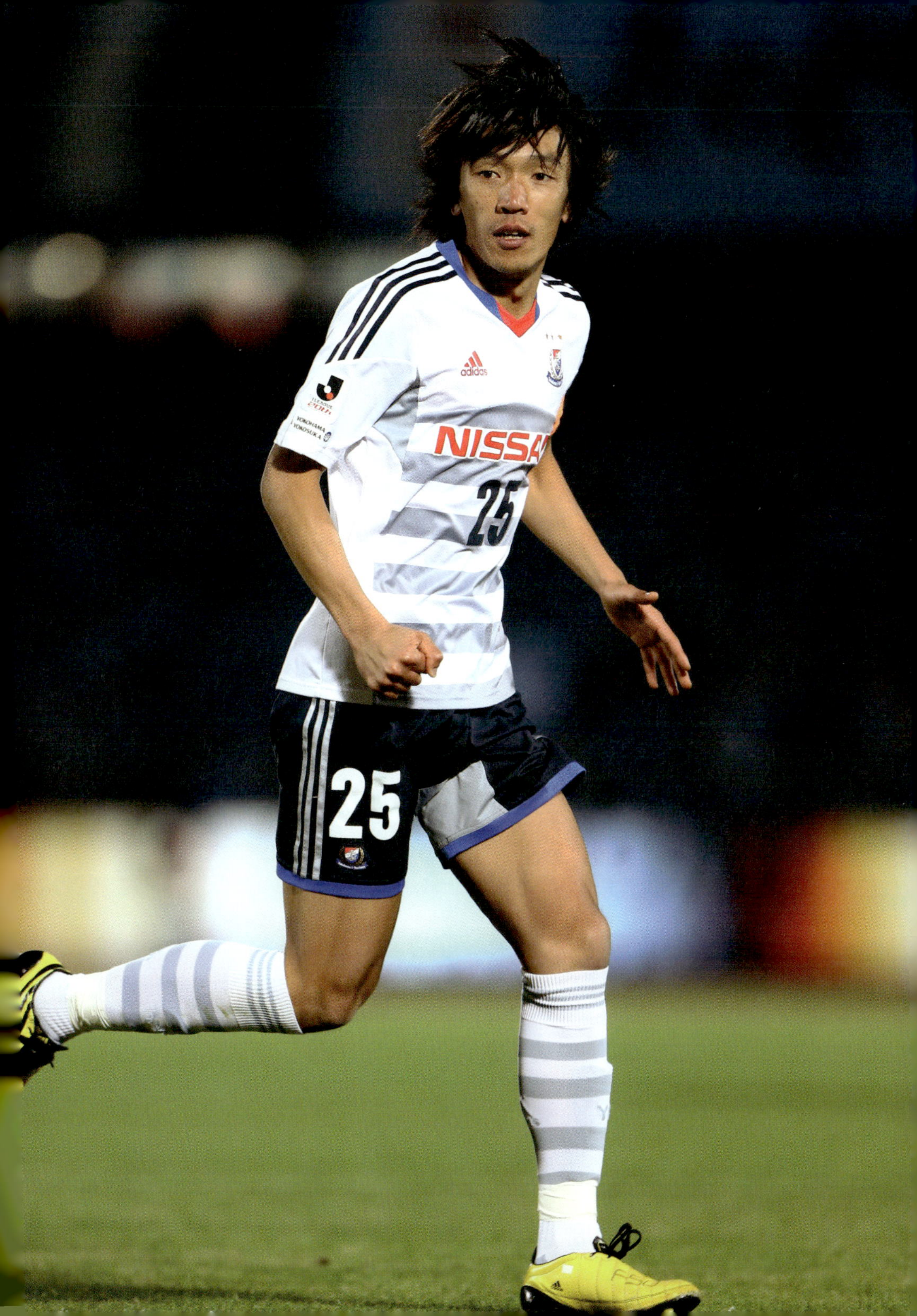
adidas
NISSA
25
25

力量を発揮するため **情報** に敏感であろう

Perk your ears up to information
that will make the most of your abilities

時間をかければよいものができる、かもしれない。けれど、時間がないときのほうが力量が問われるものだ。力量を培うためには、日々の生活で目や耳から入ってくる情報を瞬時に察知していくことも大事。家から駅に向かう途中、何かないかな？　たくさんのお店、会社があり、人がいる。そこらじゅうにヒントがたくさん詰まっている。ニュースも、自分のこととして捉えて理解しているだろうか。あらゆることを貪欲に吸収していこう。

Maybe you'll come up with something amazing if you just invest the time, but it's only when you're pressed for time that your skills are really put to the test. In order to cultivate these skills, it's also important to quickly pick up on any snippets of information that might cross your path over the course of your daily routine. All the shops and restaurants, offices, and people on the journey from your home to the train station, for instance, are rich sources of clues and hints ripe for the picking. Are you taking in the news for the day by seeing how it relates to you personally? Make sure you greedily absorb everything around you with a passion.

143

躬な人に聞こう

Ask someone nearby

素の自分を知っている家族は、最も厳しい批評家だ。デザインに対する姿勢や考え方について、どんどん批評してもらおう。一般人の客観的な視点や、生計を共にする視点からの発言は、デザインやビジネスの感覚を見つめ直すよいきっかけになる。また、ある程度デザイン案が固まった時点で、頭の中で家族や恋人を前にして、説明する自分を想像してみよう。うまく伝えられただろうか。頭をほぐして案を見つめ直すには、お薦めの方法である。

Your family knows your true self and they are your bitterest critics. Ask for their opinions about your attitude towards design or way of thinking. Opinions with objective perspectives from the general public or from someone who you live with provide good opportunities to reconsider your designs or business sense. Also, when you are at a point where your design idea is roughly taking shape, imagine yourself explaining it to your family or lover. Can you explain it well? This is a recommended method for reviewing your idea with a relaxed state of mind.

145

キュ✴︎ピッド になれ   Become a cupid

面白い化学反応が起きるであろう人たちを引き合わせてみる。そうした場を提供するだけでもいい。もちろん損得は関係ないところで。そんなことをしているうちに「架け橋のデザイン」が生まれる。

Try to connect people who might have interesting chemistry together. All you need to do is provide a place where they can meet. Of course, don't think about what you stand to gain or lose by this matchmaking process. Before you know it, you've managed to "design" yourself a position as a kind of mediator or middleman.

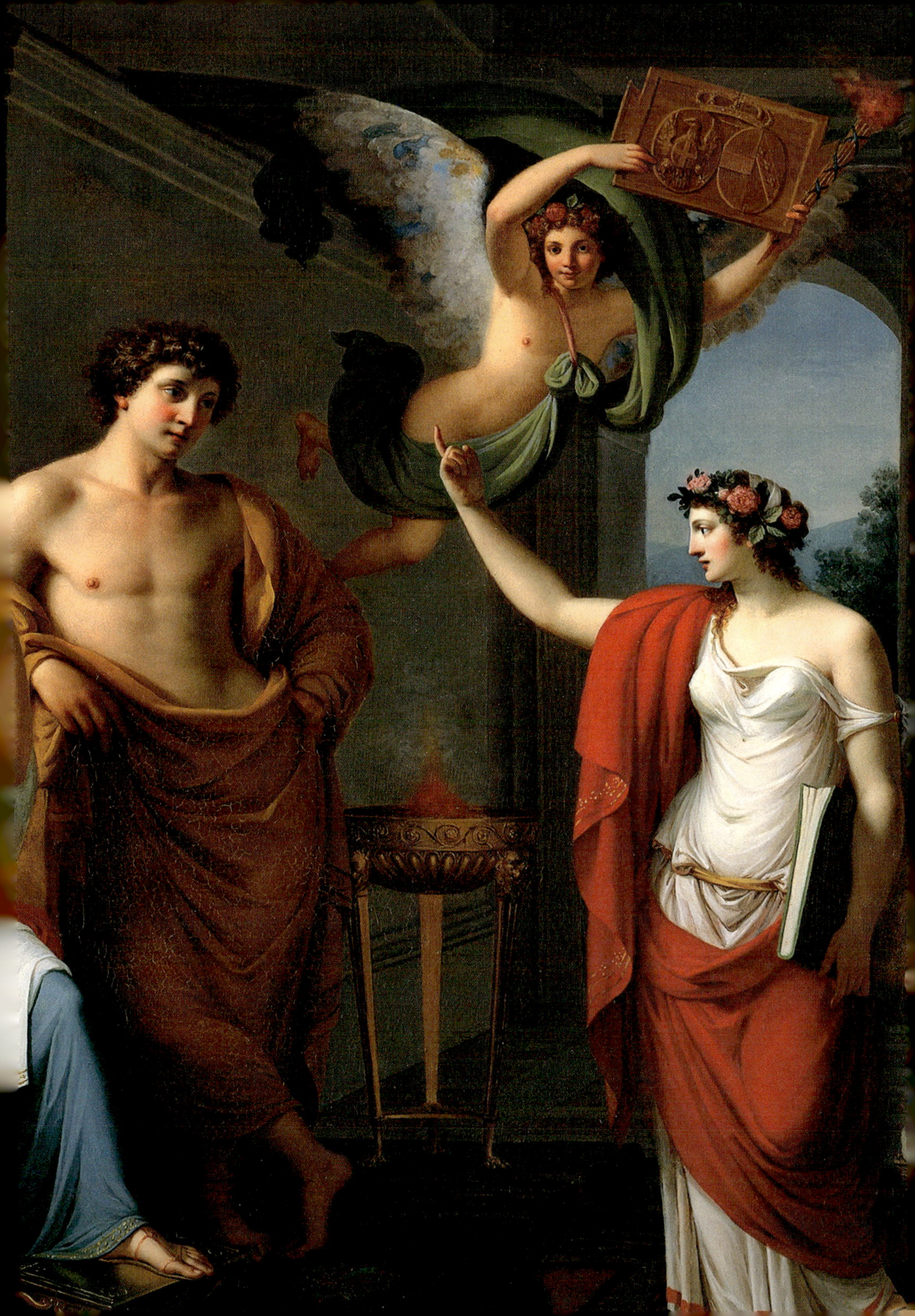

言葉で置き換えてみよう

Put it in words

仕事の対象に、ある言葉を仮に設定してアプローチすることがある。例えば写真撮影で「闇を撮る」という仮の言葉から動き出す。すると黒さのなかの階調であったり、奥行きであったり、長時間露光している時間だったりと、さまざまなアプローチが生まれてくる。写真にして言葉にしてまた写真にして。

One possible working approach is to come up with a provisional term or phrase to describe it. For instance, trying to "capture darkness" during a photo shoot. This will inspire various approaches inspired by the gradations that exist within black, a sensation of depth, or the time involved in long exposures. Take a photo, express it in words, and then take the photo again.

149

最も美しく見える状態を探そう

Look out for things at their most beautiful

洋式トイレはフタが閉じている状態が最も美しい。すべてのモノには、それぞれ最も美しく見える状態があり、あらゆる場面でその探求と実践を忘れてはいけない。美しいモノを世に送り出す役割の者は、便器のフタは用をたした後、必ず閉じなければならない。

A western-style toilet looks most beautiful when the cover is closed. All objects in this world have an ideal state that makes them look their best. As a designer, never forget that it's your job to keep searching for and implementing these situations wherever you can find them. Those whose role it is to bring things of beauty into this world should always remember to close the lid on the toilet after you finish your business.

151

実感を信じよう

Trust your gut feeling

業界の慣習には目を向けず、経験のなかから培った実感を頼りに決定する。それが非常識なことであっても、実感を通してのみ、リアルな希望とリスクを算出することができる。最も信頼できるのは実感なのである。

Decisions should be made by ignoring industry conventions and relying on gut feelings that are acquired through your own experiences. Even if it lacks common sense, you can only calculate realistic hopes and risks through your gut feelings. The most reliable thing is your gut feeling.

153

挨拶もデザイン

Greetings are design, too

人と会うときは挨拶で始まり、挨拶で終わる。弊社には、来客があればスタッフはいかなる仕事の最中でもいったん手を止めて挨拶を行うというルールがある。挨拶をしないことは来客に対する敬意の欠如であり、そのようななかからよいデザインは生まれない。挨拶は「ユアタイム、ユアペースでサービスします」というデザインの姿勢である。

Meeting someone begins and ends with a formality or greeting. One of the rules at our firm stipulates that all staff leave their work, no matter what they may be in the middle of doing, and greet visitors who've arrived at the office. Not greeting visitors shows a lack of respect for these people, which will never lead to good design. Greetings tell other people that you provide a service at their own time, pace, and convenience.

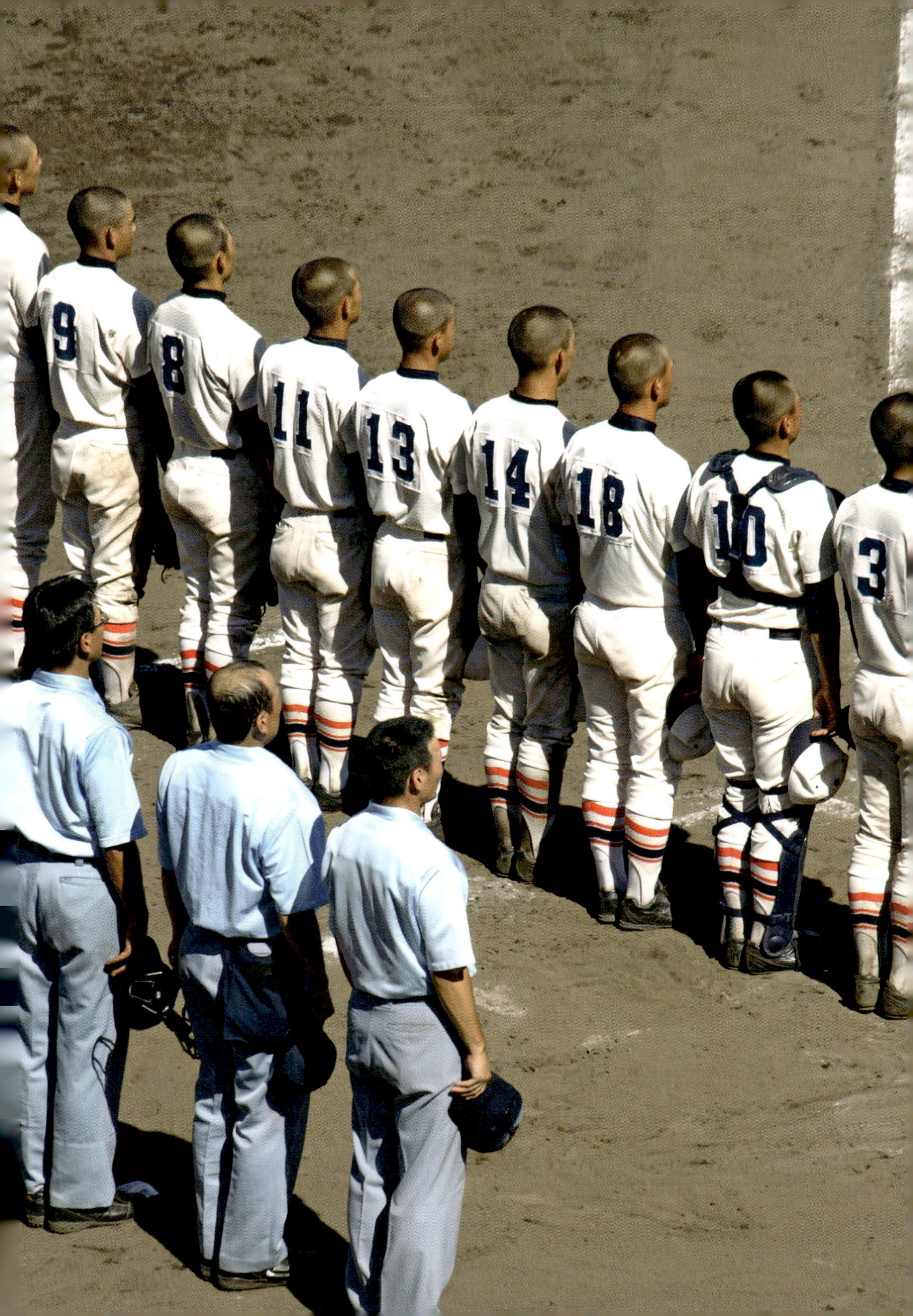

一日の計は朝食にあり

The key to a successful day is breakfast

生活の基本は体調管理。フリーランスはとかく生活が不規則になりがちである。徹夜や深夜まで仕事をすることが効率的かどうか、立ち止まって考えてみよう。早起きしてしっかり朝食をとることで、1日をポジティブにスタートすることができる。朝食で、生活と仕事のリズムを整えよう。

Keeping in good shape is the foundation of life. Freelancers tend to have irregular schedules. Stop and think about the efficiency of working all night or late at night. By waking up early and eating breakfast, you can start the day in a positive manner. Regulate your life and work rhythms by having breakfast.

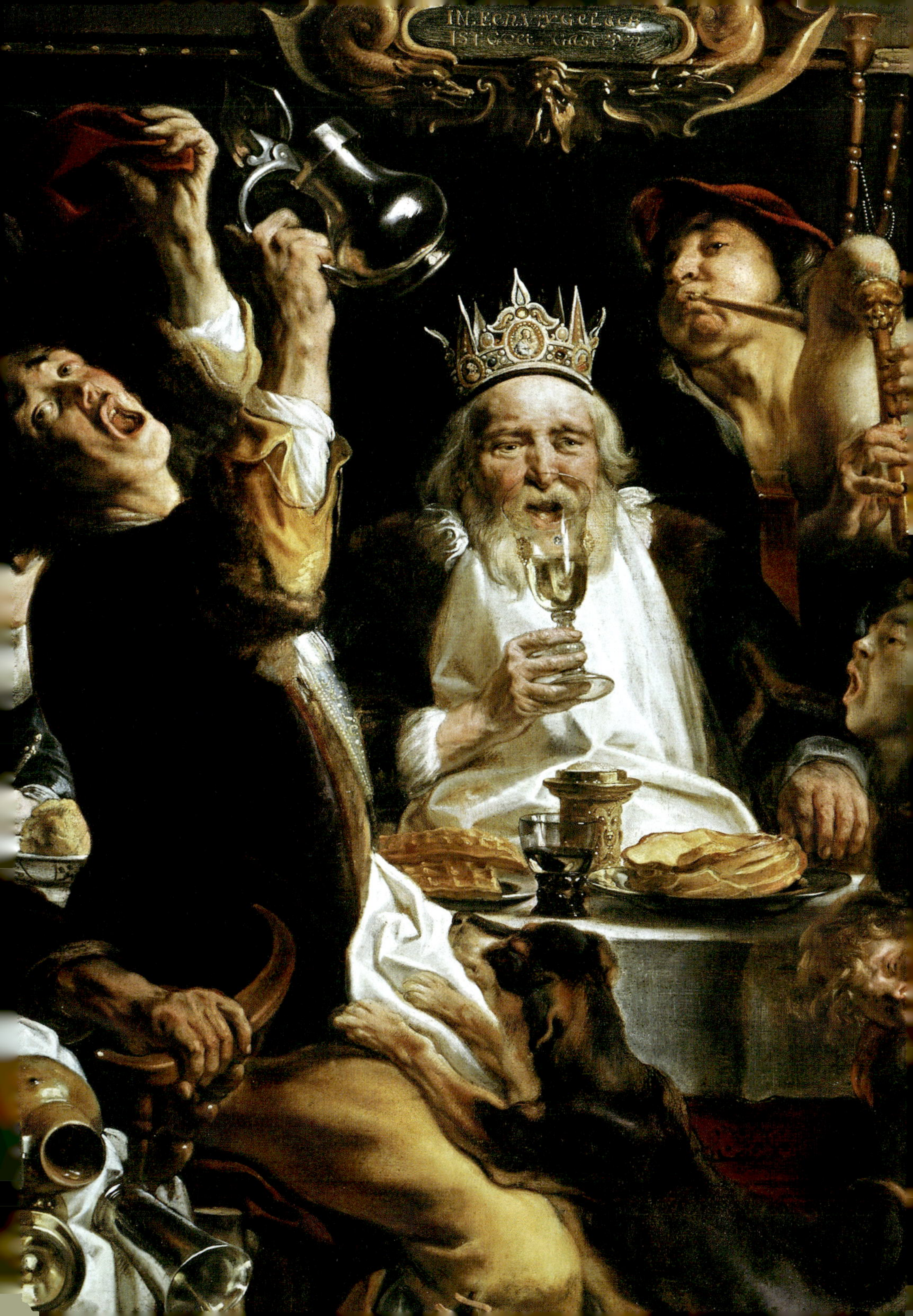

顧客本位であれ

Be customer-driven

「顧客本位」とは決して「顧客迎合」を意味する言葉ではなく、「自分本位」ではないところからはじめるデザインの基本姿勢である。いかに素晴らしいデザインであっても、人々に受け入れられない一方通行のものであるかぎり、それは本来のデザインとは呼べない。相手の存在を感じながら創造することが重要であり、暮らしのなかで生きてこそデザインたり得る。

Obviously, "customer-driven" doesn't mean that you should be ingratiating. On the other hand, avoid striking out on your own at all costs when it comes to design. No matter how wonderful your design is, if it's just a one-way thing and not accepted by other people, you can't call it "design" in the strict sense. Make sure to create things with your client or end user in mind. Design comes about by living in the real world.

159

あえて若手中心のチームをつくろう

WAKATE

Create teams of mostly young people

経営者やベテランスタッフはこれまでの経験上、知識も豊富で失敗の少ない手堅い結果を残すことは可能である。でも、過去の成功にとらわれがちで、新しいことにチャレンジする気持ちは薄いかもしれない。そこで、あるプロジェクトでは全員若手のチーム構成で進めてみるのもよいだろう。特に基幹事業があれば、それを任せるのである。そのほうがその基幹事業は長続きするかもしれない。マンネリが一番の敵なのだから。

Thanks to their previous experience, managers and veteran staff members may be able to deliver solid results with few mistakes by putting their extensive knowledge to use. But they tend to stick to their previous successes, and may not have the inclination to take on a new challenge. So maybe it's a good idea to deal with certain projects using a team made up entirely of younger staff. This is particularly true if the mainstay of your business is in good shape – you should just try leaving it to the youngsters. This way, your core business might even prosper longer. The worst fate of all is to get stuck in a predictable routine.

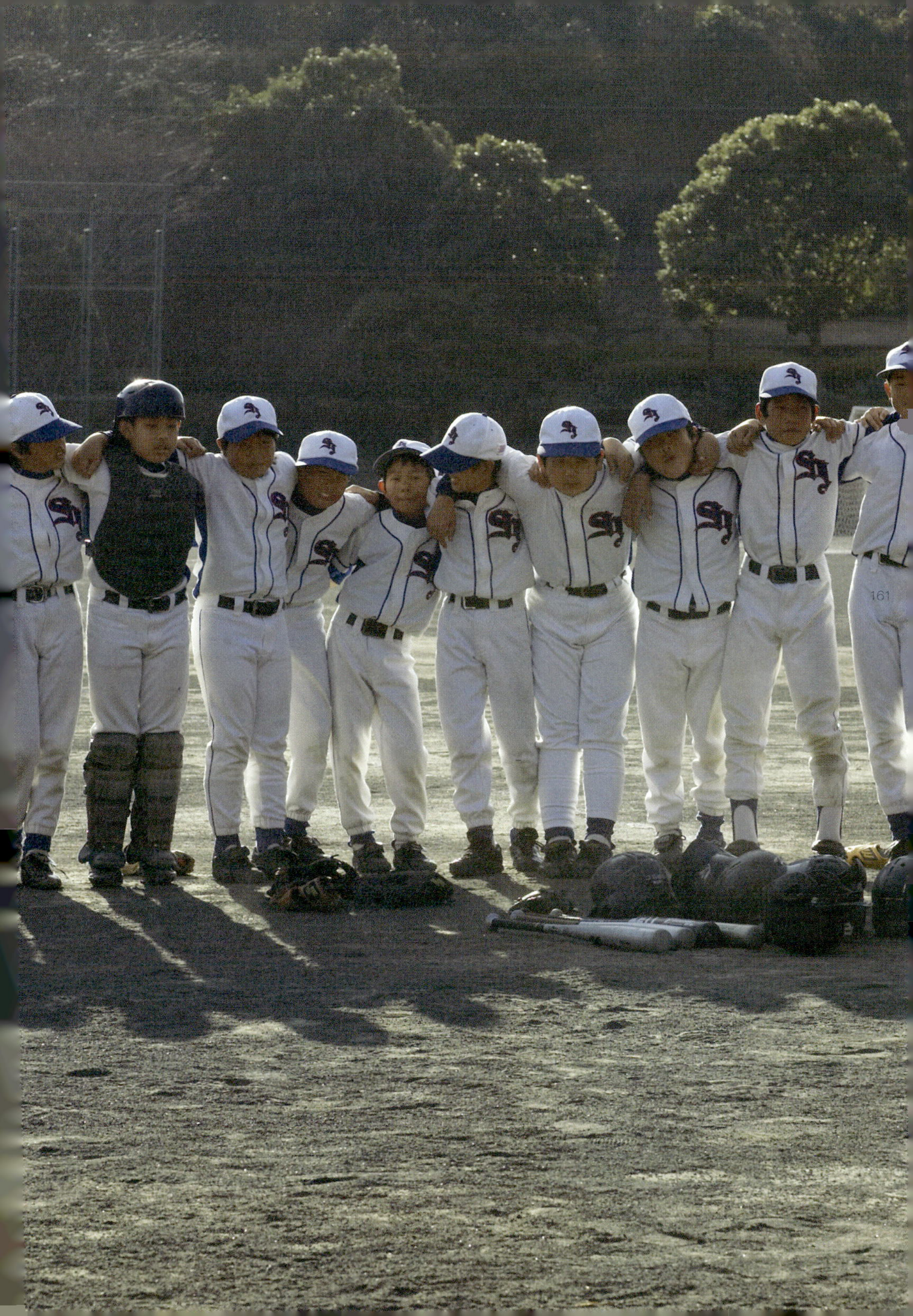

母になる

Become a mother figure

女性は仕事一筋で生きるよりは、1度は母になってみてほしい。異なる世界をもつことでバランスがとれるだけでなく、デザインは生活に密接に関わっているわけだから、違うチャネルをもつことが多いに役立つ。そして母がもつ優しさと強さは偉大である。それをもって仕事ができればきっとどんな場面も切り抜けられるはず。

Instead of devoting yourself wholeheartedly to your work, what women really want is for you to try and see what it's like being a mother. Becoming a mother gives you a fine balance between various elements because you have access to different worlds, and design bears an intimate relationship to life itself, so being attuned to different "channels" and wavelengths goes a long way. The tenderness and strength of a mother are noble qualities to have, as well. If you can tackle your work with these traits on your side, you shouldn't have a problem dealing with even the toughest of situations.

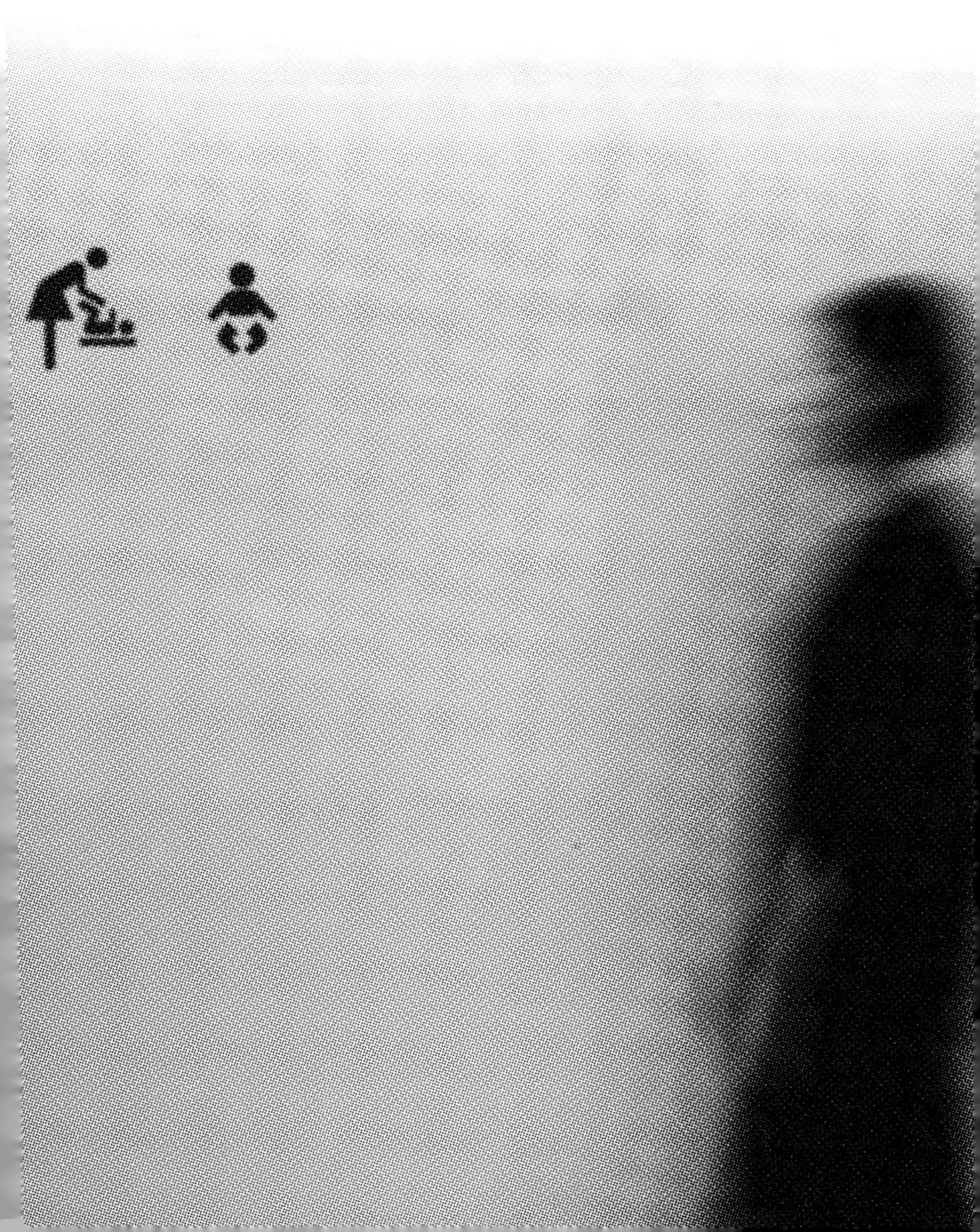

物語をPRせよ

Sell those stories

デザイナーは物語をPRすることに知恵と創造力を注ぐべきであり、これは一定期間継続して行う必要がある。数多くのプレスと関わると「デザインの見られ方」が重要であることに気づく。それらの総体が、ブランドとして表現される。自身のデザインを通して、他者の評価を観察し続けること。キーマンからのアドバイスや批評は確実にデザインに反映されるので、長い付き合いがなにより大切だ。

Designers ought to devote their knowledge and creativity to launching PR campaigns that will drum up public interest in stories, in a continuous way for a fixed period of time. Dealing with lots of press and media people will make you realize the importance of how design is seen and regarded. All these things are expressed in the form of a brand. Keep an eye on public opinion through your own designs. Advice, feedback, and appraisals from the key players in the industry will definitely been reflected in your design work, so a long and lasting relationship with them is essential.

THE
GODFATHER

1972

会食をデザインしよう

Design the meals you have together

会食はデザインである。クライアントと食事をしているときはあえて仕事の話はしない。お互いがどのような人間であるかを最も試されている最中だから、あくまでビジネス抜きで接する。食事中にコミュニケーションが取れれば、食後のミーティングは概ねうまくいく。クライアントは信頼を与える準備段階として、私たちと食事をするのだ。

Food is design. Make sure you don't talk about work whenever you have dinner with your clients. These occasions are when you're trying your best to find out more about each other as individuals, so leave your business persona at the door. If you can have a lively conversation during the meal, the meeting that follows will typically go well. Your clients are having a meal with you as a preliminary step to entrusting their concerns to you.

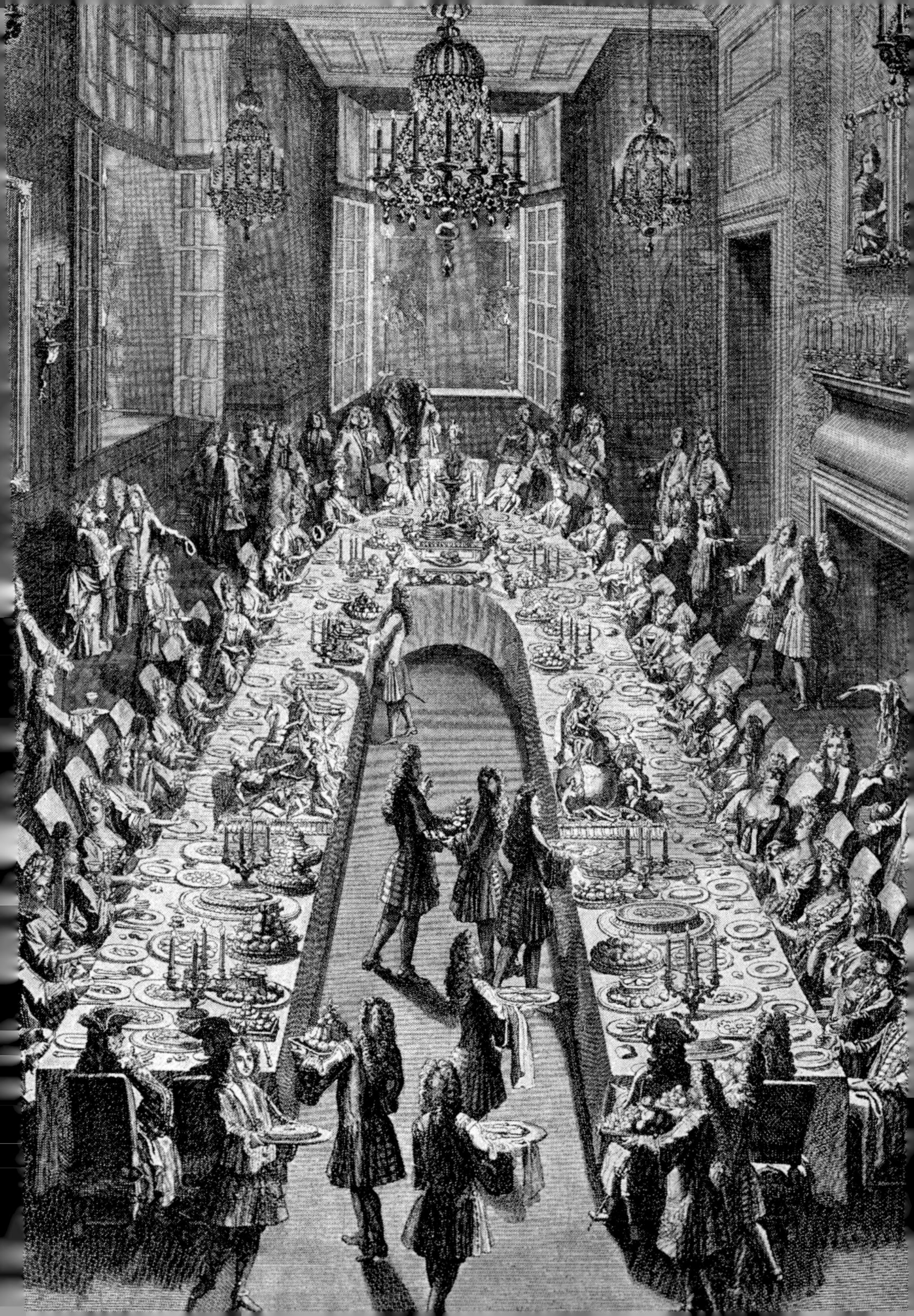

沈黙

しない

Don't keep

silent

結論を出すことが目的か、議論することが目的かをはっきりさせて会議を行う。結論を出す場合は、出すまで終えない。議論の場合は、沈黙しないというのがルール。「今考え中です」と言いながら何も話さない人がいるが、ほとんどの場合は何も考えられていないか、発言する勇気がないだけ。セッションの機会に瞬発力を鍛えていこう。

Hold meetings with clear objectives — are we here to reach some kind of conclusion, or talk things over? If it's the former, don't end the meeting until you reach the conclusion. If the latter, make sure nobody stays silent on the matter. Some people are going to refuse to contribute and say "I'm still thinking about it", but most of the time they haven't thought about it at all. Use these sessions as opportunities to train your staff to perform when put in a tight spot.

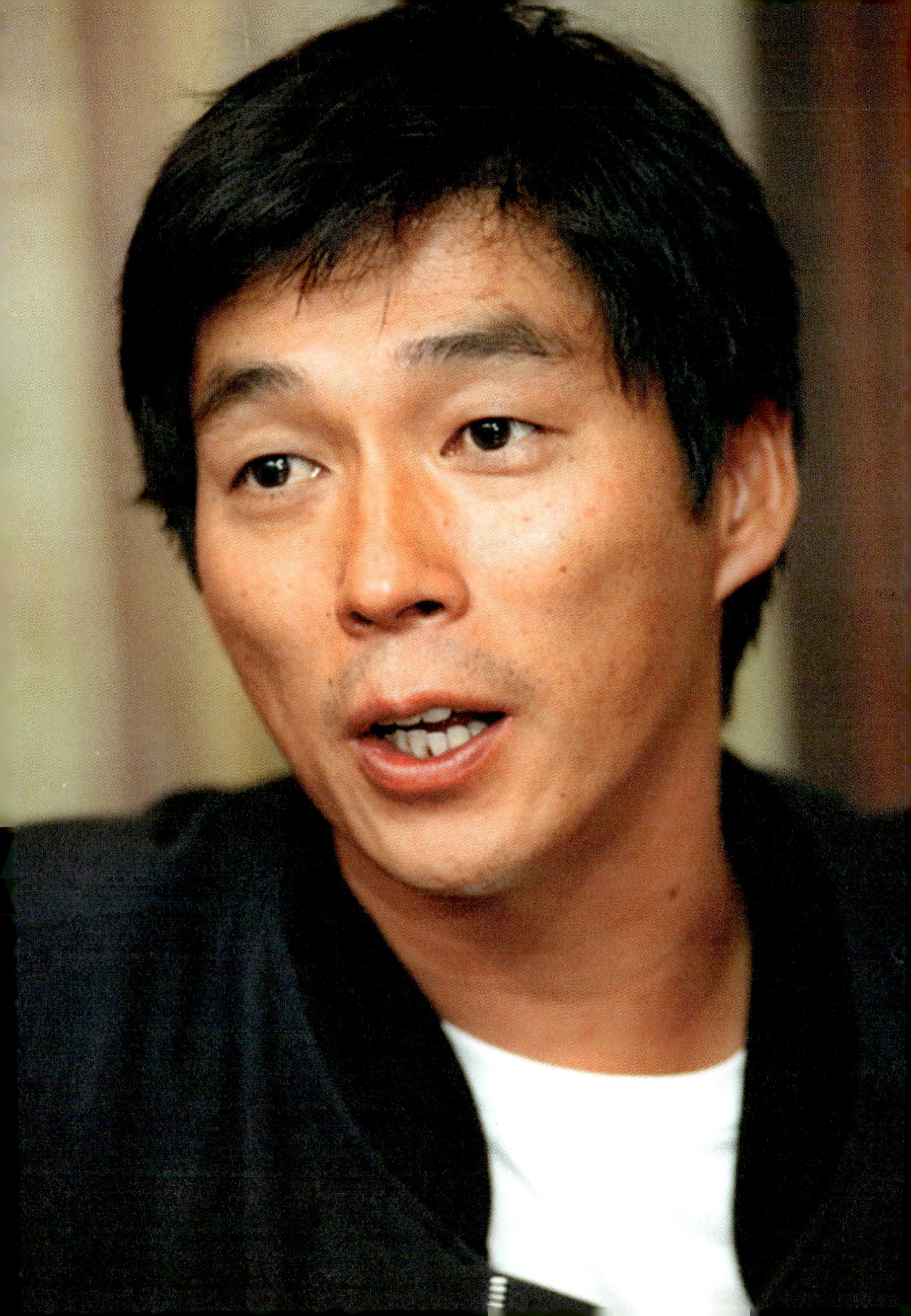

不特定多数へ発信はしない

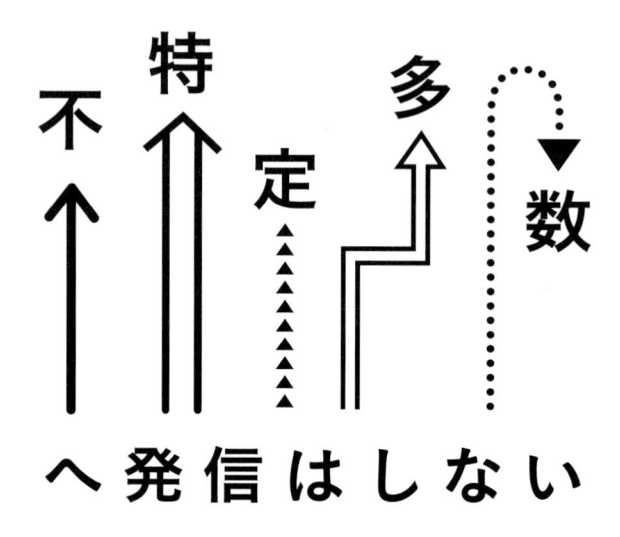

Address a specific audience

マスプロダクトでなく、ニッチなサービス業という仕事柄にあっては、不特定多数への発信を行わない。結果としてはそれがフィルターとなり、いい仕事に恵まれる。

A niche service that is not a mass product shouldn't speak to a general audience. The nature of your work ultimately serves as a filter, and gets you the choicest jobs.

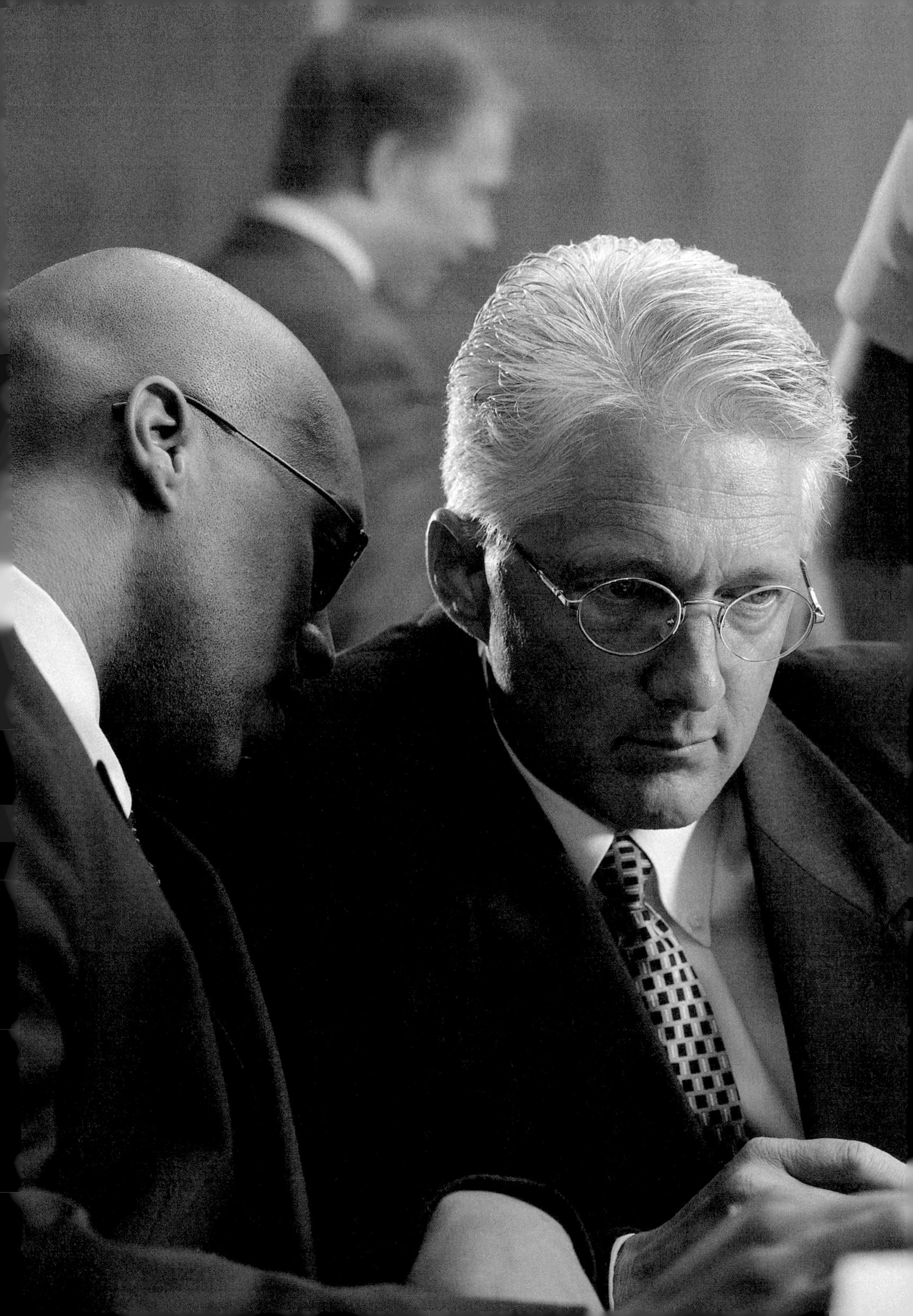

オリジナリティを検証しよう

Verify originality

情報や流行は頭のなかに自然とインプットされている。もしとてもよいアイデアを思い付いたとしても、ほかのデザイナーも思い付いている陳腐化したアイデアという可能性が高い。そのデザインにオリジナリティが宿っているかどうか、あらゆる角度から検証することが重要だ。そして、オリジナリティを持ったデザインだけが、長く生き残ることができる。

Information and trends are naturally absorbed by your mind. Even when you come up with a wonderful idea, it is highly likely that the idea has already been used by another designer and has become obsolete. It's important to verify from all sides to see if the design has originality. Only designs with originality can endure for the long term.

173

仕事は美しくあれ

Make beautiful work

完成度の高い仕事は「美しい」。デザインやアートの世界だけでなく、どんな仕事においても、完成度の高い仕事は、美しい。

Highly polished work is beautiful. This applies to all sorts of work, not just the world of art and design.

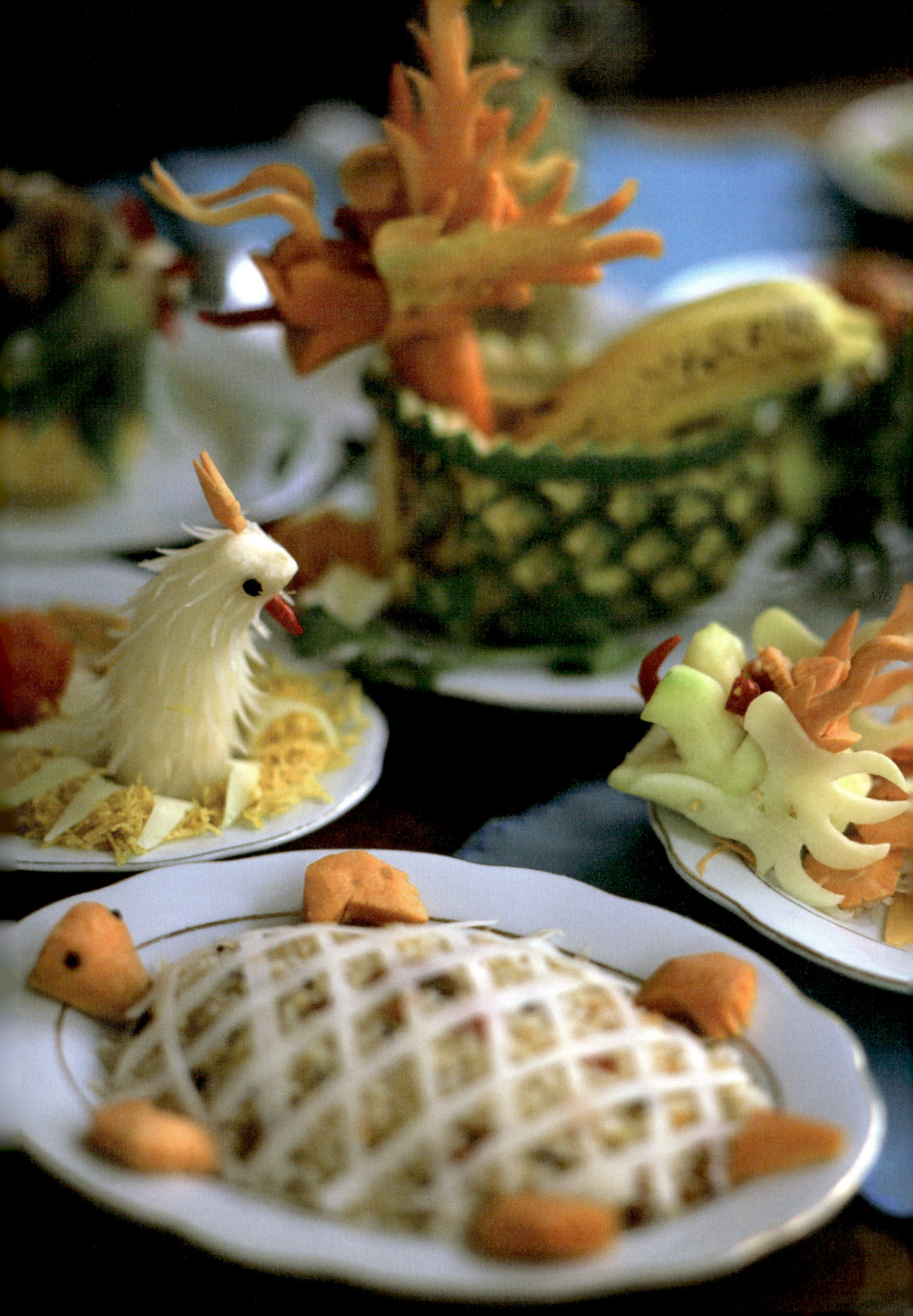

仕事をする人とは仲良くしよう

Become friendly with those you work with

仕事をする人と仲よくなれば、必ずよい仕事ができる。反対に、人としての理解が不足したまま仕事を続けると、トラブルが起こりやすい。仲よくなるには時間がかかるが、信頼を失うのは一瞬である。たっぷりと時間をかけて、人と人の付き合いから始めるのがデザインである。

If you can become friendly with those you work with, you'll definitely be able to produce good work. Conversely, you're going to run into problems if you keep working without understanding these people at a personal level. While it takes time to get friendly with someone, you can lose someone's trust in a single instant. Design entails investing that extra bit of time to create interpersonal relationships from which your work will emerge.

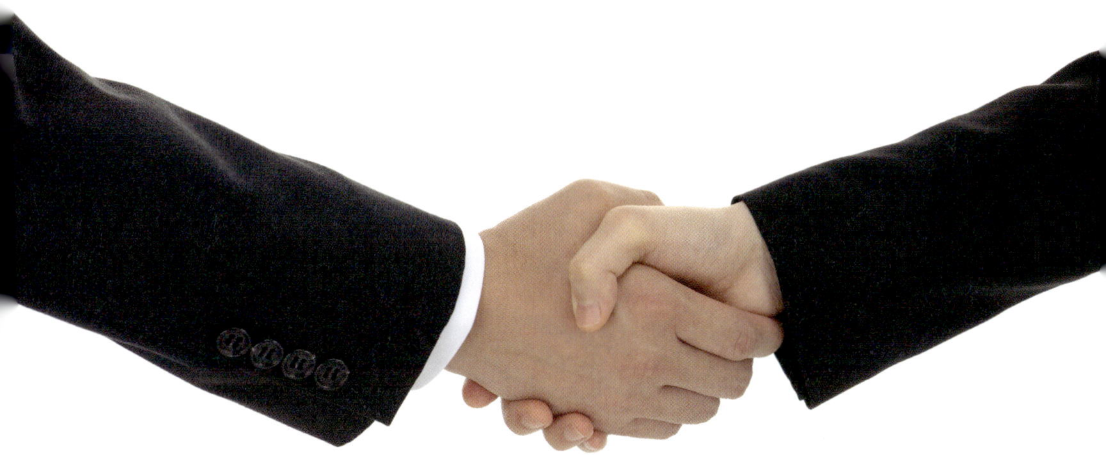

約束の時間の 10 分前 に到着しよう

Arrive 10 minutes ahead of time

ミーティングやプレゼンテーションの場の空気を先制することで、その日の切り札になるような思わぬアイデアがひらめくこともあるし、見えていなかった問題が見えてくることもある。時間に遅れて、謝る言葉からスタートすることだけは絶対に避けなければならない。

Never misjudge the appropriate scale of the organization required to maintain the quality of your work. The moment the number of staff exceeds a certain limit, the standard of their work is going to nosedive. In order to maintain the quality of work expected, you need to find an ideal size and scale for your organization that corresponds with the content of the work and the abilities of your managers.

179

粗密のバランスをもたせよう

Strike a balance
between the coarse and fine

最近の消費者は本当に必要なものしか買わない。特に紙離れの激しい書籍の分野ではなおさら。そうなると内容はもちろんのこと、デザインでも「役に立ちそうな感じ」を出すことが求められる。そこで、誌面をわざと粗密が混在するようにつくる。粗な部分は読みやすく、目の留まりをよくして内容のよさ＝わかりやすさを出し、密な部分で情報量の多さ＝役立ち感を出すのである。これで売れるとは限らないのが難しいところだが……

These days, consumers only buy what they absolutely need. This is even truer when it comes to books, which are moving away from paper at an alarming rate. Content now becomes a non-negotiable given, while the design of these books needs to appear useful and functional. When designing for paper, therefore, make sure you intentionally include a blend of coarse and fine textures. The coarse parts are more legible and make it easier for the eye to latch onto the text, emphasizing the quality of the content. The fine print, so to speak, conveys the volume of the information presented, and a sense of being functional and helpful. Of course, this approach doesn't necessarily mean that the title will sell...

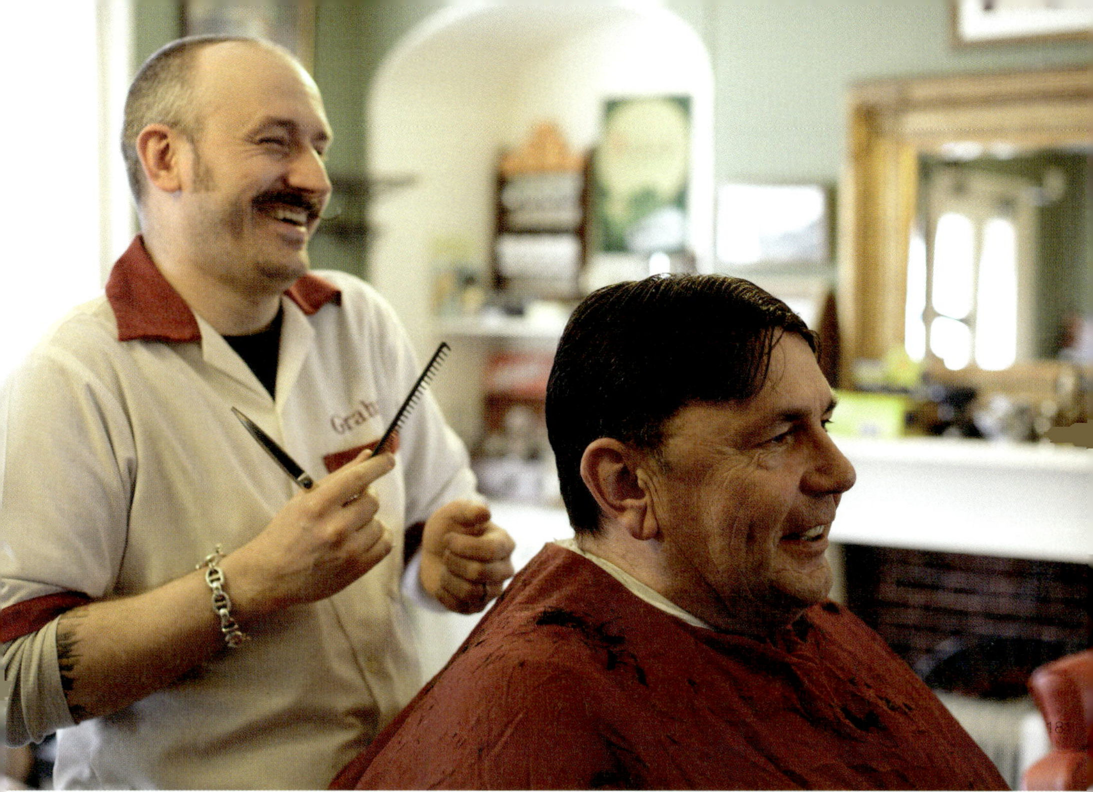

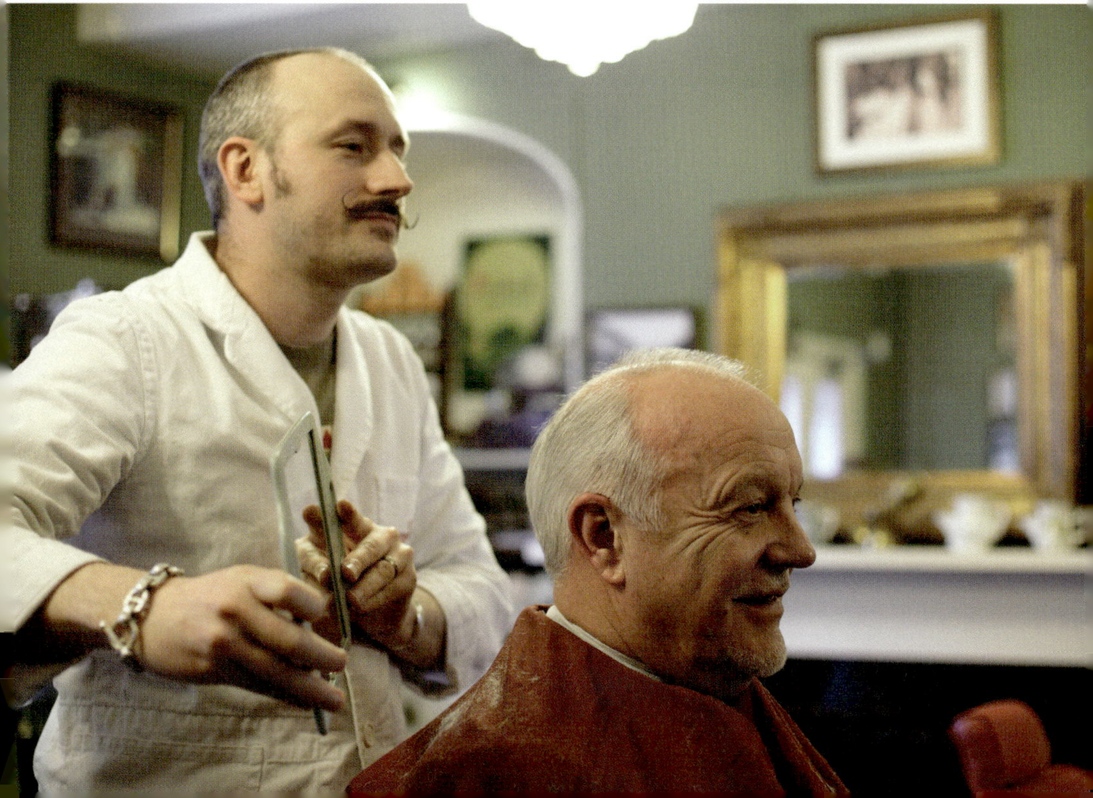

代替[?]法
を考えよう

Find some other way

自分で言うのもなんだが、スケッチは下手だから描かない。また、下手なものだから実物と違う気がしてならない。スケッチを練習するのも1つの方法だが、自分は別の方法をとった。正確な図面を描き、完成形を想像できるような訓練をした。時間がかかり間違いも多かったが、今では身に付けた1つの技術として活用している。

It's kind of embarrassing, but I can't draw to save my life and so I never make any sketches — or I do, but they always end up looking totally different from the real thing. Practicing how to sketch is one possible way of doing things, but you decided on a different method. You made an accurate diagram, and trained yourself to be able to envision the final product. It ate up a lot of time and you made lots of mistakes, but now you've acquired this skill that you can deploy in your work.

183

異なる「時間」への思いやりをもとう

Pay attention to different forms of "time"

1つの建築物ができるまでの長い時間。締切を中心に動いている編集者の時間。24時間オンであり続けるボスの時間。日本と海外とでは、時差はもちろんのこと、異なる時間の価値観…。ビジネスにおいて、自分の時間とは違うさまざまな時間の流れがあることを知っておくことは有効である。異なる時間体系のなかで動く仕事や相手への配慮ができれば、円滑でスムーズな関係を維持し、無駄なトラブルを回避することができる。

There's a time difference between Japan and other countries, of course. But what about value systems associated with different conceptions of time? The length of time it takes for a single building to be completed, for instance. The time of an editor with his mind always on his deadlines, or that of a boss who is always "on" twenty-four hours a day. When doing business, it helps to bear in mind that time flows in all sorts of ways, many of which obey a different rhythm to your own. If you respect the different paces at which each of your clients and projects operate — all of whom have their own conception of time — you'll be able to keep things going smoothly and avoid any unnecessary problems.

185

感情をぶつけて本音を伝えよう

Let your emotions show

笑顔も大事だけど、きちんと話せないと、伝えたい事も伝わらない。謝るのに、感謝するのに、メールではなく顔を見て直接言おうよ。恋愛映画観なよ。泣く、笑う、怒る…。感情をぶつけようよ。ケンカしよう。物わかりのいい人もいいけど、いい人どまり。お互いにぶつかって本音をさらけ出し、反省しよう。そうすれば、相手の気持ちを考えられるんじゃないかな。

It's important to smile, but you won't be able to make yourself understood if you can't speak freely. Don't apologize or thank someone in an email — express your feelings directly, in person. Shed tears, smile, get mad, just like in a romantic movie. Let those emotions show. Quarrel and argue. People who listen and empathize are nice, too — but they're just "nice". You need to get to grips with other people, hold nothing back, and then reflect on it. That way, you'll really understand how the other person feels.

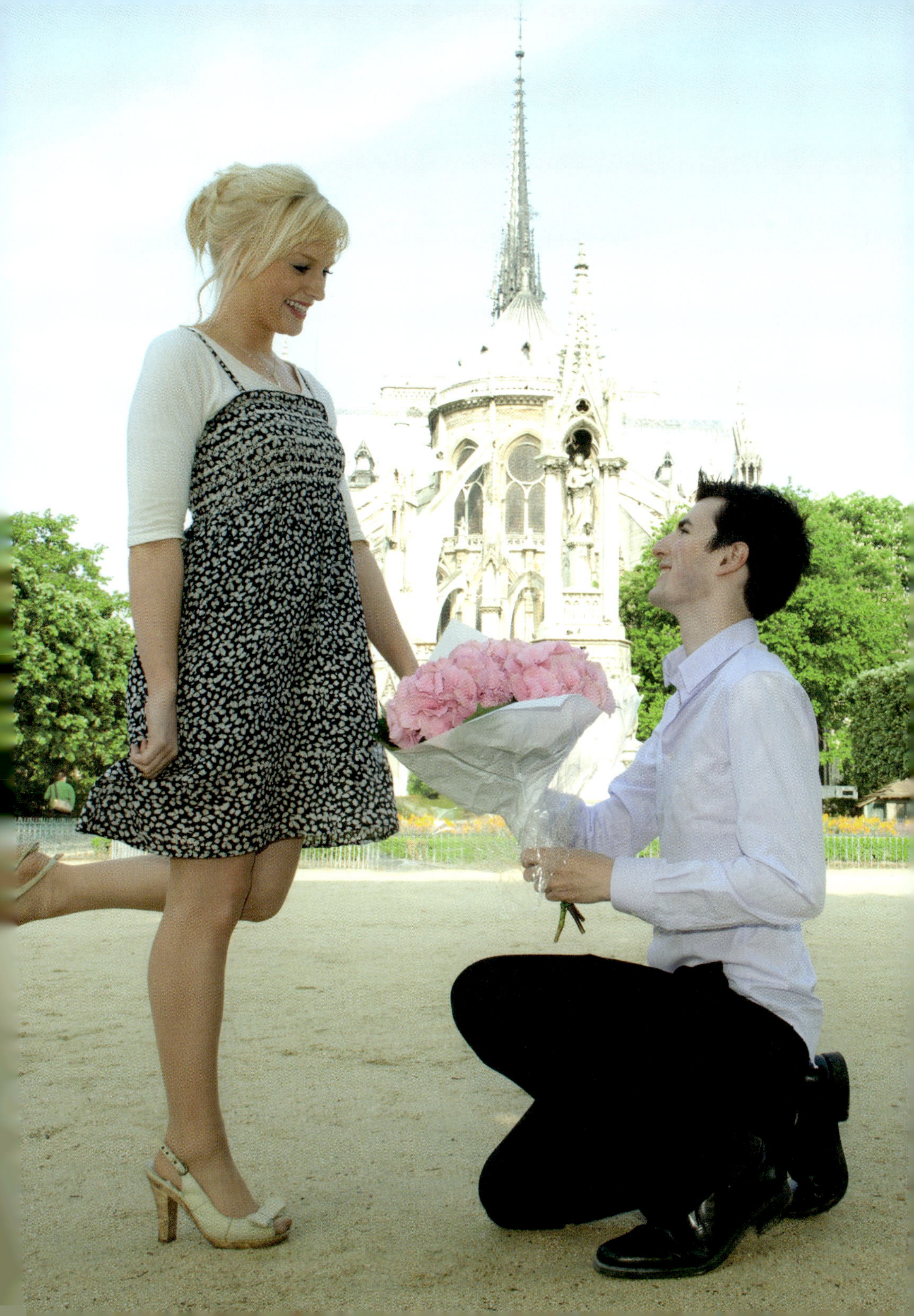

格好良さは 70%にとどめよう

Stop at 70% for the cool factor

デザイナーは常にカッコイイものを求めがちであるが、エンドユーザーにとって、デザインの先進性は理解されにくい面が多々ある。カスタムメイドの製品ならクライアントが納得すればそのデザインは◎なのだが、マスプロダクトになると、高感度な人から鈍感な人まで多数の人に受け入れられるデザインが求められる。そこで製品化する際には、70%程度の格好よさになるようにする作業が必要になる。ある意味、角を丸める作業である。

Designers tend to always be on the lookout for cool stuff. For end users, though, many of the more innovative aspects of design can be tough to get a hold on. Custom-made products can be said to be well designed as long as the client is satisfied, but products made for a mass market need to appeal to all sorts of people – both connoisseurs with refined tastes and sensibilities, and people who are completely insensitive to design. In order to turn an idea into a viable product, you need to make sure that it's "only" 70% cool. This often involves softening the "edginess" of the product, so to speak.

30% OFF

小間切
118
299
35
税込価格(円)

自分を綺麗に輝かせよう

Make yourself look good

キレイってステキ。美容を怠らずに、いくつになっても綺麗でいたい。美しく見えることに損はないよね。

Everyone likes attractive people. Don't skimp on that beauty regimen — make an effort to look good no matter how old you are. It never hurts to look attractive.

191

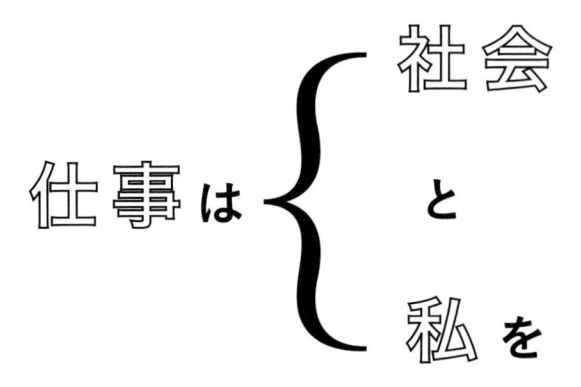

仕事は ｛ 社会 と 私 を ｝ つなぐものと考えよう

Work is something that brings you closer to society

仕事がなかったら、と考え不安になる１つの理由はまずお金。ただし、お金が入れば何でもよいというわけでもない。どのように社会と関わりたいか、関われるかのかたちが結果として仕事となったらいい。仕事とは他人に捧げる時間、その時間が長短をもって還ってくることで自分が生き還る。

Money is one of the main reasons why people become anxious about having no work to do. But it doesn't mean that anything goes as long as you have the money. Ultimately, the goal is to do work that addresses the question of how you want to be involved in society, and the specific things that you can accomplish. Work is about dedicating your time to other people. The strengths and weaknesses associated with that time will be returned to you in kind — a sort of karma or payback.

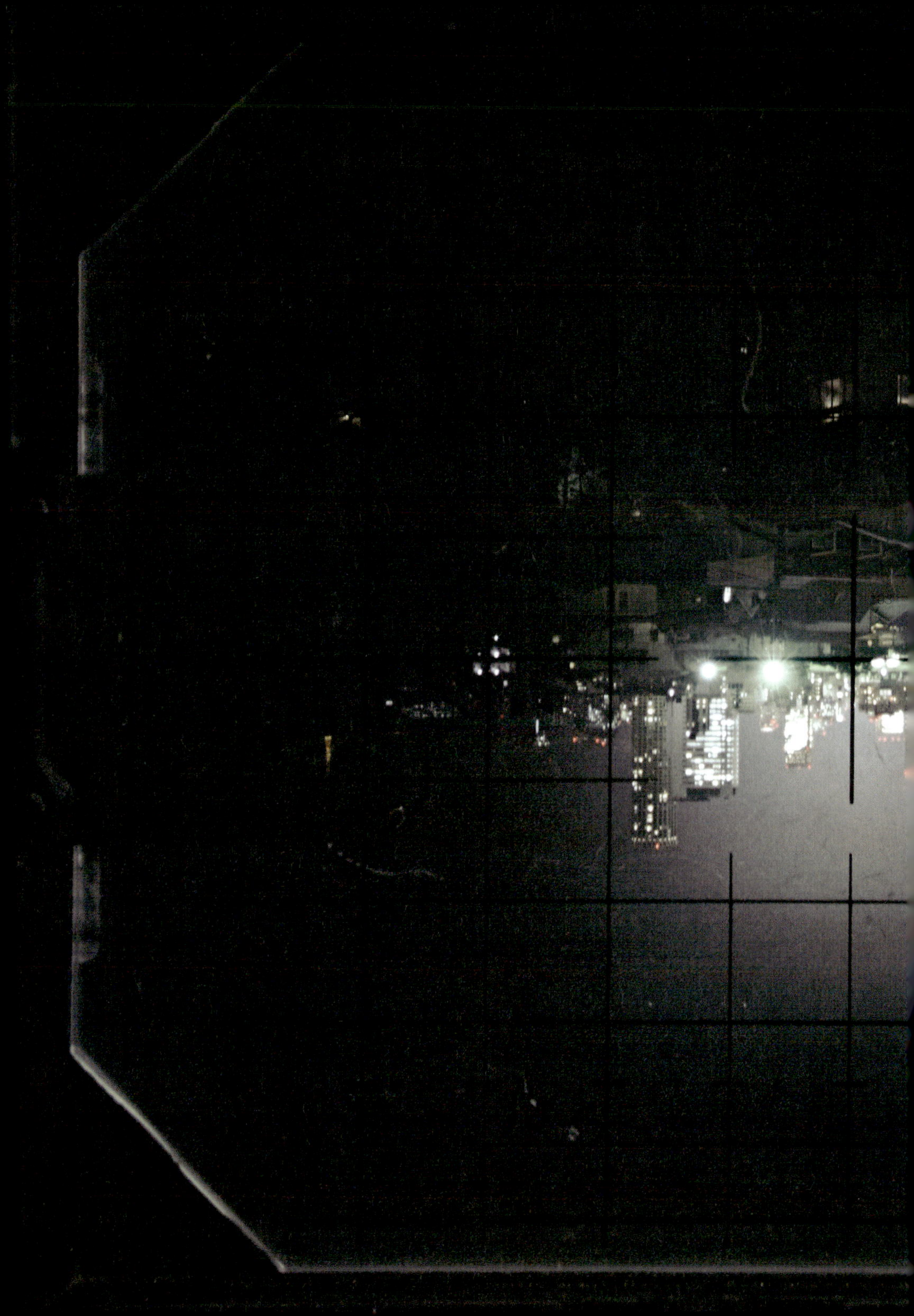

2017　　2016　　2015　　2014　　2013

できることの　ちょっと先を考えよう

In 3 years

Think about
overreaching a little bit

社会人になりたてのころは、よいアイデアを持っていても、人脈も、実現するためのお金にも恵まれることはそうはない。今やりたいと思っていることは、実は3年後にようやく実現できることだったりする。まずは自分自身の置かれている状況を冷静に考えること。そしてそこから少しだけ背伸びしてチャレンジしてみる。その積み重ねが、次のステップへつながる。

Even if people have a wonderful idea right after beginning their career, they usually lack personal connections and money to realize the idea. The idea you want to work on now might be realized after three years. So, calmly consider the situation you are in, and then challenge yourself with things that are a little bit out-of-reach. The layers of such challenges lead you to the next step.

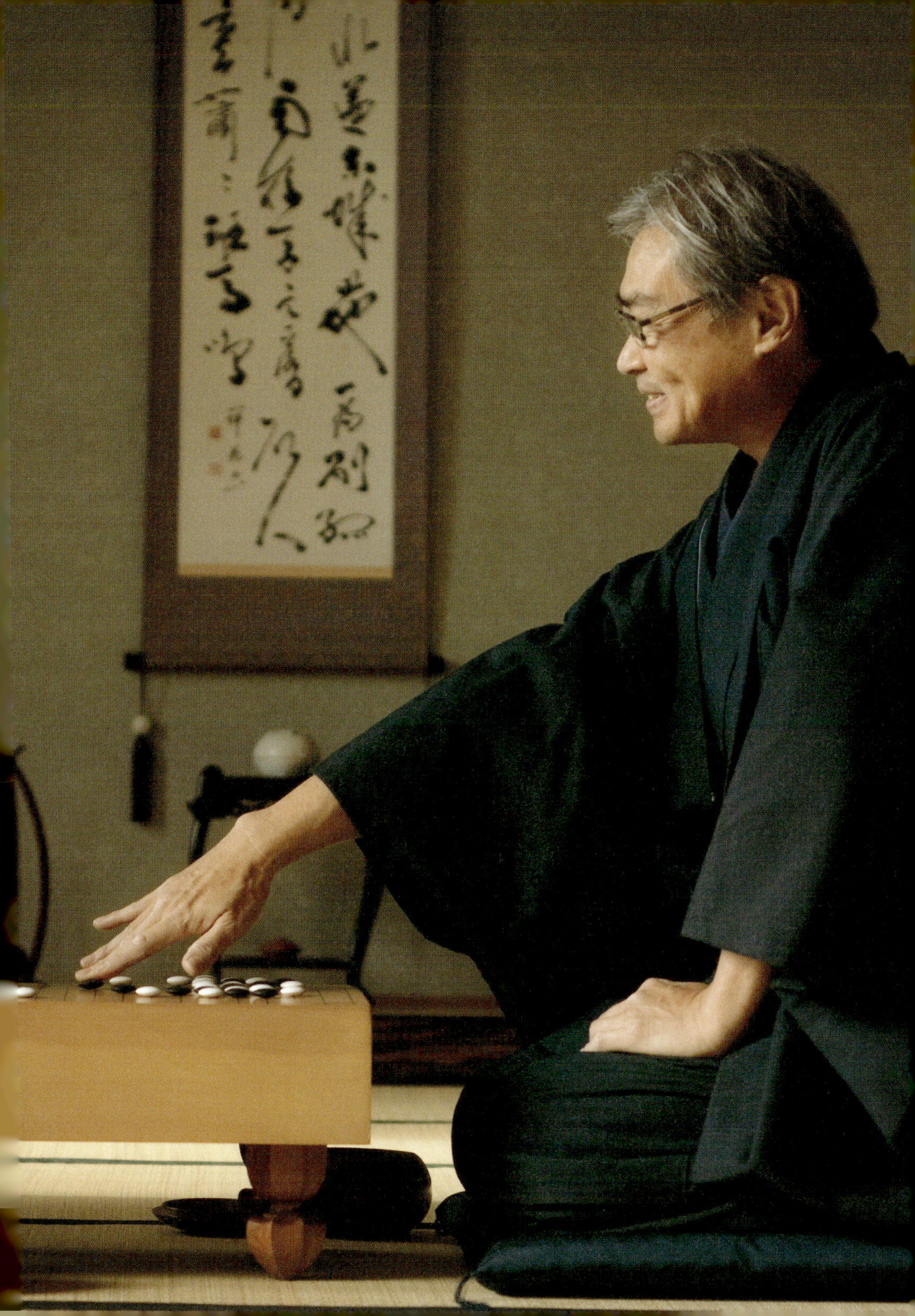

name まずは名前を付けよう！

Decide on a name first

プロジェクトチームを発足したら、まず最初にするお仕事は、自分たちのチーム名を付けること！　自分たちのチーム名も決められないような人たちに素敵な未来はない。一体感が増し、責任感も出てくるし、なによりもメンバーのテンションが劇的に変わる。

Once you get your project team up and running, your first priority should be to pick a name. A team that can't even decide what to call themselves doesn't have a very bright future ahead of them. Choosing a team name will bring members together and make them take responsibility for the task, dramatically lifting the spirits of your team members.

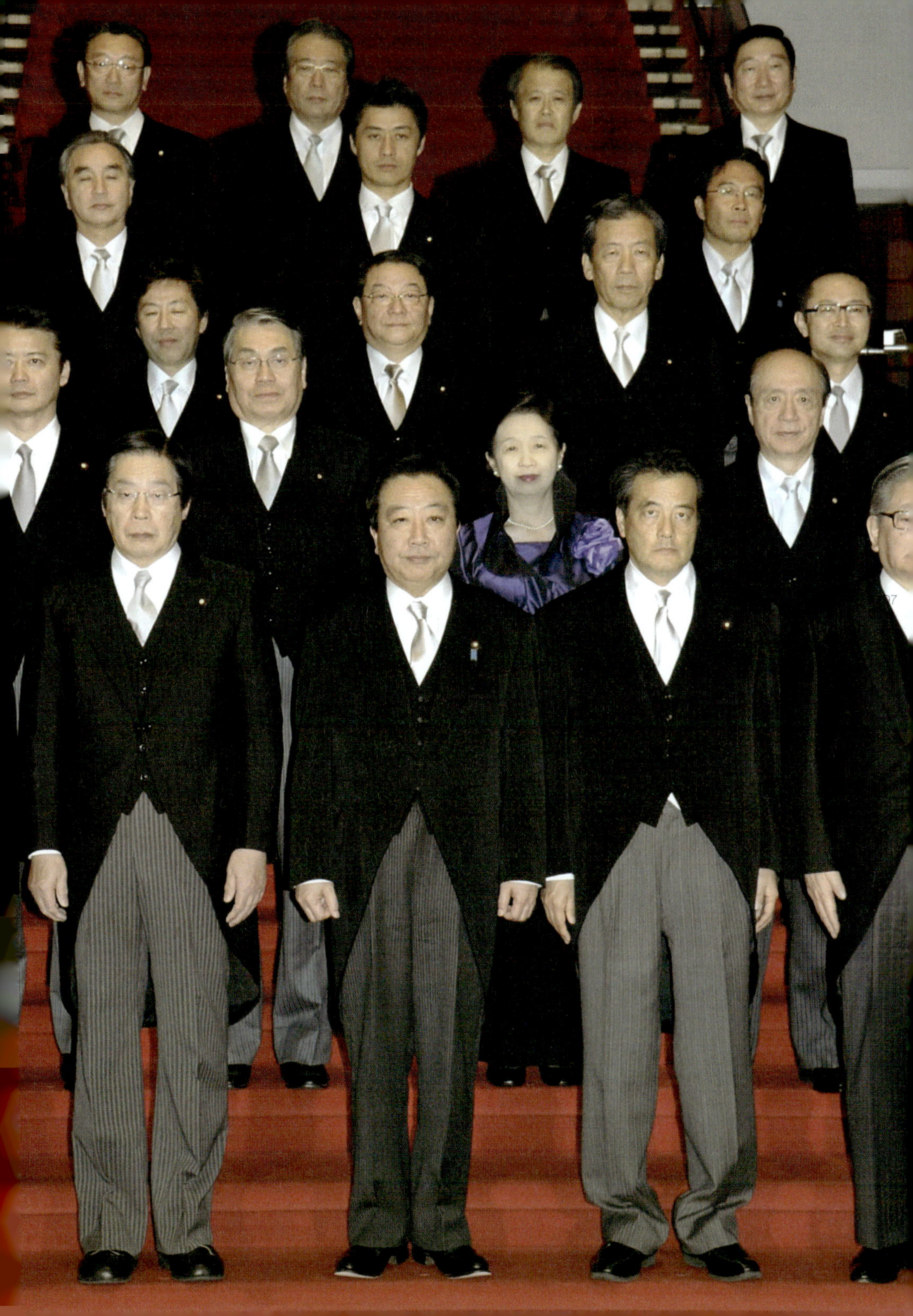

不意打ち
をかけよう

Launch a sneak attack

待ち合わせ場所から打ち合わせ場所に行く短い時間。打ち合わせ場所について席に座ってから、お茶が出てくるまでの合間。世間話のように言いにくい話をしてしまおう。あるいは聞きにくい話を聞いてみよう。「構え」のない「素」が引き出せる時がある。

You have just a short window of time before you proceed from your meeting point to the place where your meeting is going to be held — a short interval after you arrive at the venue and sit down, but before the tea is served. I tend to make small talk that might be slightly awkward, or offer a listening ear to someone who might want to say the same. The answers aren't going to come rolling off the tongue, but they will get the message across.

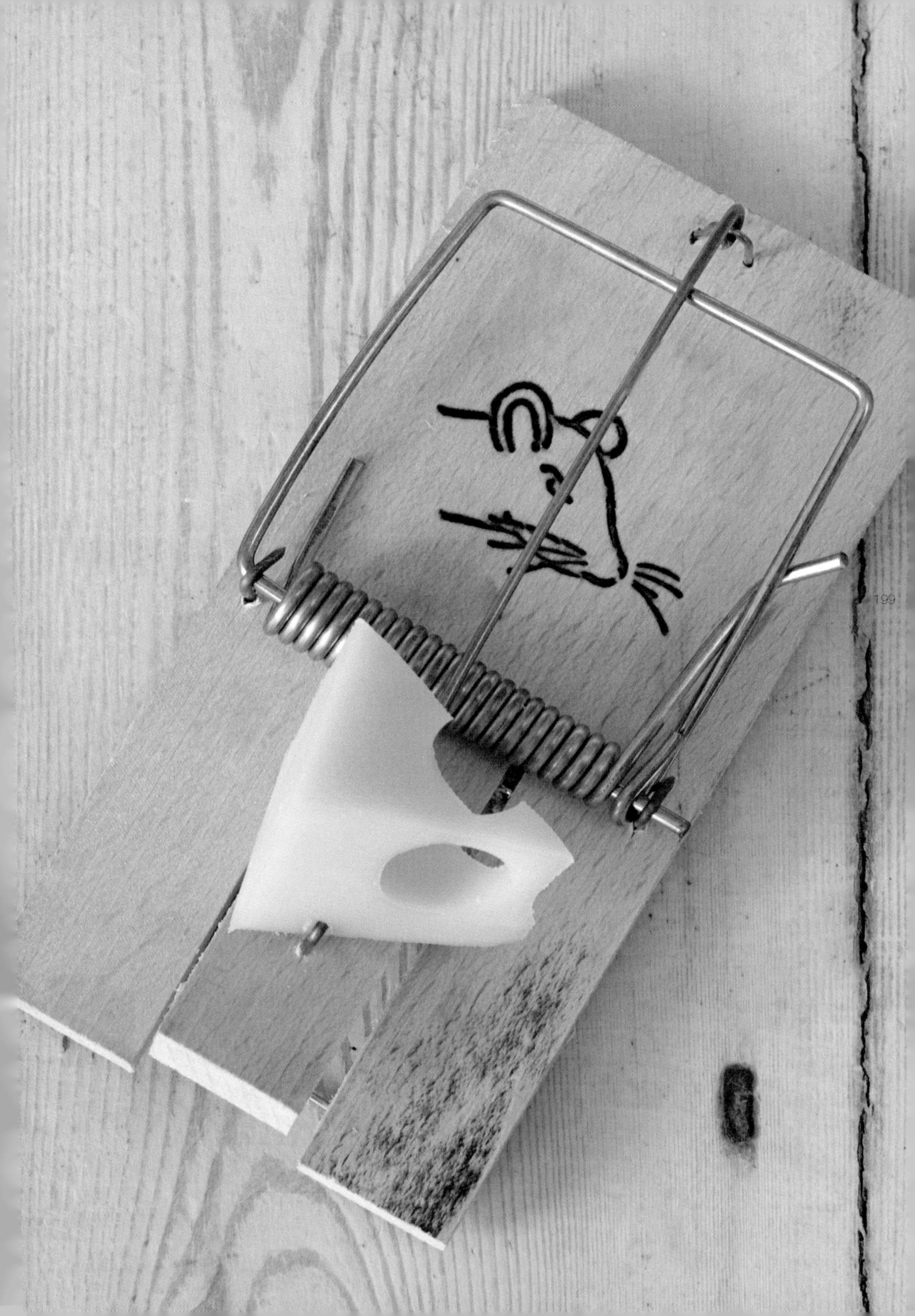

製品名
を目立たせよう

Find a name that stands out

パッケージは製品の顔である。何が目立つとその商品と一目でわかるか、ほかの製品と差別化ができるかを考えることが重要になる。デザイナーは格好いいグラフィック要素と格好いい欧文のフォントを目立たせがちであるが、ここは日本。日本語でしっかりPRできていて、かつ格好いいデザインになっていることが求められる。

The packaging is the face of your product. Find out what about it needs to stand out, so that consumers can recognize it instantly, or distinguish it from other products.Designers tend to resort to nifty graphic elements or cool-looking European fonts to make their work stand-out, but this is Japan. You need a solid PR campagin in Japanese in addition to a cool design.

北海道産
本ずわい
がに 3,000円

プロダクト として捉えてみよう

Consider it as a product

若者がファッションデザイナーを志す動機として「自分の着たい服をつくりたいから」という意見をよく聞く。そしてもちろん人によるが、デザインの核となる経験を身に付けずにその初期衝動のままつくり、自己満足で終えてしまう人も多い。まずは服を「プロダクト」と捉えてみよう。設計図（パターン）と素材（生地）で服は完成する。その基礎を学んだうえで「自分のつくりたい服」を考えることが大切である。

An often heard reason for young people to become fashion designers is, "I want to design clothes that I want to wear". Although it depends on each person, many of them create with such early intentions but lack experiences that become the center of the design, and as a result they only please themselves. To start with, just consider clothes as "products". Clothes are made with patterns and materials. It's important to think about "clothes that you want to make" only after learning the basics.

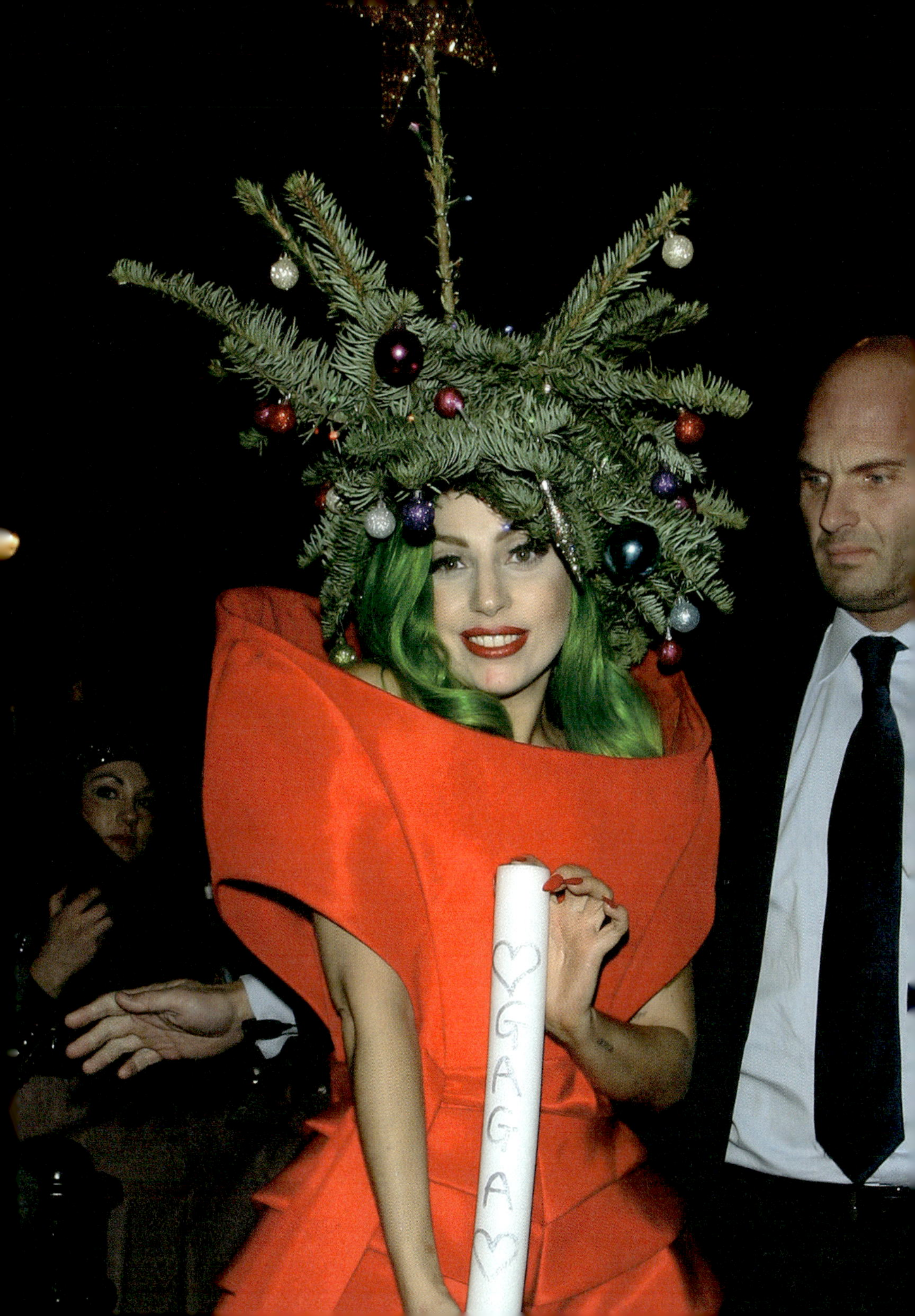
GAGA

見通しのよいところで見てみよう
Get your bearings where the view is better

仕事は何度も迷うもの。何度も曲がり、方角を失いかけたら一度大きな道に出よう。見通しのよい道で、改めてランドマークを見つけ、そこに向かって歩こう。

You're going to lose your way many times. If you start to lose your way after making too many turns, get out of there and make your way out to the main road. Find some landmarks where you have a better view of things, and make your way towards that direction.

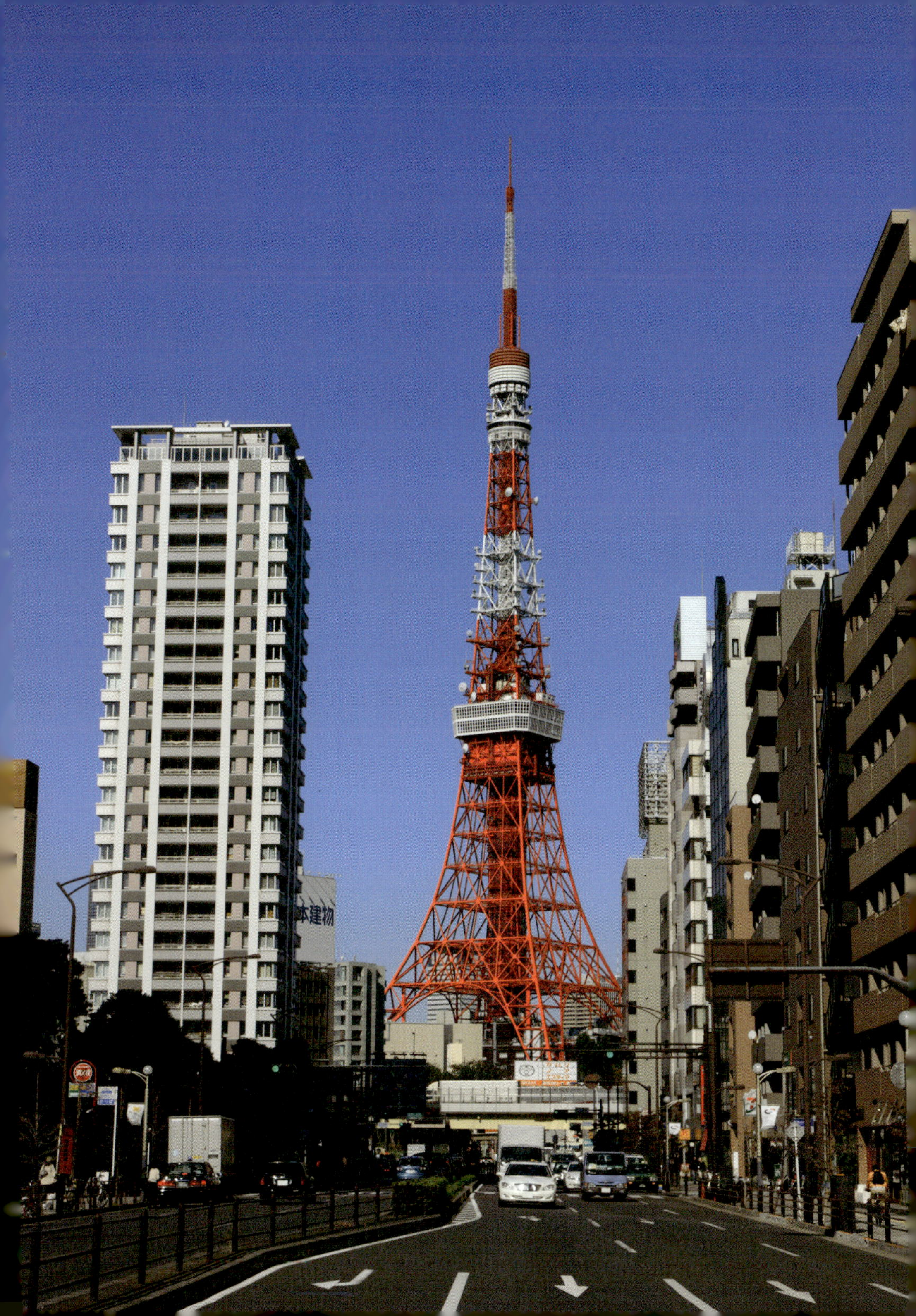
本建物

見えないものに
価値を与えよう

Assign value to what
you cannot see

見えないものに与えられたかたちを、さらにかたちにする。写真に被写体を収めるというのは、そのようなことである。まだ見えていない、かたちになっていない物事をさまざまな条件を読みほどき着地させる。それがすべてではないが、1つの見方を与えるのも仕事の1つである。

Take invisible things that have already been given a form, and imbue them with yet another form. This is analogous to the act of capturing a subject through photography. Learn how to decode the various parameters pertaining to objects and things that aren't yet visible, or which haven't taken on a palpable form, and nail them down. This isn't necessarily crucial, but one of your jobs is to make obvious a particular perspective and viewpoint.

2.8 2 1.4

1.4

旅をしよう

Travel around

インターネットで簡単に情報を手に入れられる時代だからこそ、時間をかけて旅をする。旅をすると、経験やある種の情報は簡単には手に入らないことを再確認できる。

Precisely because it is an age when information can easily be obtained through the internet, spend time for traveling. By traveling, you can reaffirm experiences and certain kinds of information that can't be easily obtained.

209

賛辞を述べるような
仕事をしよう

Create work as if you were
paying someone a compliment

被写体はすでに目の前にある。そのあるもののなかから答えを出すのが、建築写真撮影の仕事。相手の仕事が無事終わりを迎えたことへの賛辞を惜しみなく述べるように、その撮影の姿勢は肯定的であるべきである。

The subject's already in front of you. Eliciting an answer from within it is the job of an architectural photographer. The act of photographing that subject ought to be affirmative in a way that allows you to shower unreserved praise on a piece of work that has been completed without a hitch.

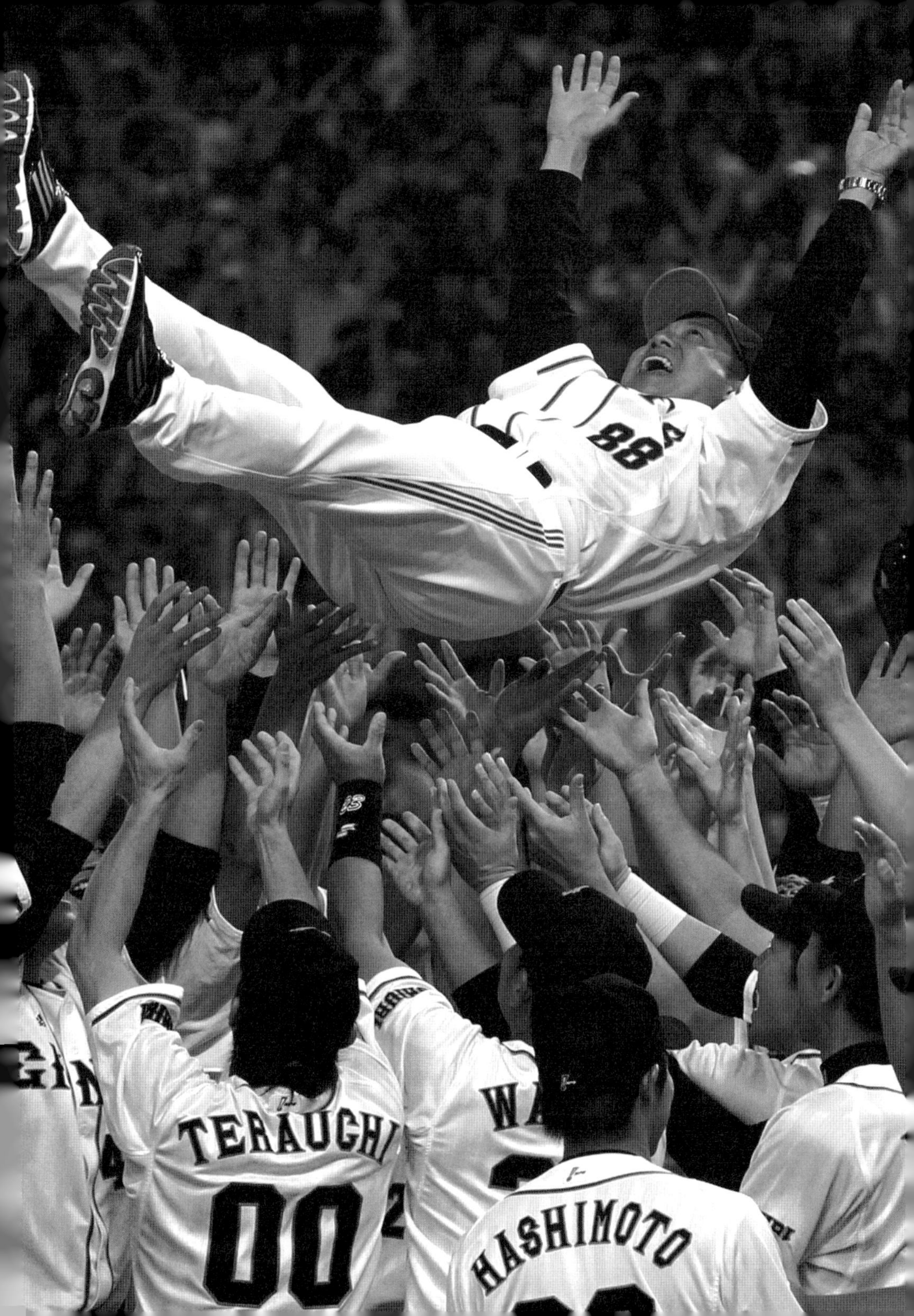
88
TERAUCHI
00
HASHIMOTO

Today's high

今日の最高は
明日の最低ラインにしよう

Today's best shot is tomorrow's
minimum requirement

今日うまくできたことは明日はもっとうまくやらなくては
ならない。一度できたことは二度目は失敗してはならない。
そう教わってきた。何より重要なのは今日自分がどこまで
できたのかという把握であり、それを復習することで明日
が生まれる。

It's not always the case that tomorrow is going to turn out better than today. But there are going to be superiors who believe that you should do a better job the next morning for things than you can do today — and have become particularly attached to their little slogan. Naturally, you want things to turn out better than they stand today. In order for that to happen, you need a clear idea of how well you did today.

213

問1から問5までの設問を据えよう

Rank key challenges from 1 to 5

クライアントの希望を、5問に分けた1つの設問にしてみる。簡単なものを問1と問2に。その応用を問3・問4に据える。問5は総合的なもの。順番通りていねいに進め、簡単な問1が解けると自然と問2も解ける。その2つの答えを利用して、問3・問4に向かう。難しいが、それが解けたらするりと問5も解け、結論に至る。はじめにクライアントの希望をよく聞き、読み解く順番を決めるのも大切なプロセス。

Whittle your client's demands down to a single issue that can be divided into 5 points. Address the simple things with the first two points, and the practical issues involved in points 3 and 4. Point 5 is the conclusion. Take care to solve each of these questions in turn — if you manage to solve number 1, the solution to number 2 will come to you naturally. You can then use the answers to these first two issues to tackle 3 and 4. Even if they're a bit trickier, solving 3 and 4 will allow you to address number 5 without a hitch, and lead you to your conclusion. Deciding how to tackle these issues in the right order after listening to your client's requirements is an important process.

... the washing……洗濯物と...
...〜を引き抜く
... and plastic bottles……カンやプラスチックやらペットボトル
... knees……両ひざが悪い
... the snow……除雪する
...〜を植える

文の内容に合うように、次の(1)と(2)の英語に続けるのに...
う1つずつ選び、その記号を書きなさい。(各3点)

Yuina saw a house on her way to school,

ア　and its garden had no weeds then.
イ　and she knew that no one lived in it
ウ　and her father knew who lived
エ　and then she saw an old w...

打ち合わせは 自分のオフィスに招こう

\ Hello ! /

Have meetings at your own office

オフィスは、デザインの姿勢を表わすメッセージそのものである。打ち合わせは自社に招こう。口頭でいろいろと説明するよりも、直に見てもらうことで伝わることのほうが圧倒的に多い。そして、オフィスの選択にはバランス感覚が現れる。自分が千代田区を事務所の立地として選択しているのは、東京の中心で全方位のクライアントと偏りなく仕事ができるからである。また、地方や海外に容易に飛び出せるスタートポジションであることも大切である。

Your office sends a message to other people about your attitude to design, so invite clients over for meetings. Rather than explaining everything orally, your message gets across much better by having your clients see for themselves. Your sense of balance and judgment shows in where you decide to locate your office. I chose to base my firm in Chiyoda Ward because it's in the center of Tokyo, so that I can work with clients in every direction without being biased. Being here also gives me a good starting position that offers easy access to locations outside Tokyo or overseas.

仕事を限定しない

Don't limit your scope

名付けることで、仕事を限定してしまうこともある。例えば、カメラマン、写真家、写真師、フォトグラファー。呼び名はさまざまだが、あえて別な呼び方を考える。また、普通に行っている小さなことを積極的に行うことから派生する活動もある。広範囲な活動の結果がその人の個性となり、結果としての呼び名となればいい。ひるがえって、呼び方を改めて設定することから展開する仕事もあるのではないか。

Using names and labels like "cameraman" or "photographer" can sometimes place unnecessary limitations on your work. There are lots of titles out there, but make an effort to think of something different. There are also activities and projects that emerge because you've taken a more proactive approach to dealing with little everyday things. The results of a wide-ranging practice become trademarks, and hopefully bywords or calling cards associated with that person. Your career and future projects might flourish even more just by reconsidering the terms you use to refer to yourself.

鳥村 鋼一
Photographer

① 段 ② 取り ③ を ④ 大事に ⑤ しよう

Make proper plans

上司に頼まれたこと、期日や期限が決まってるものをすべて紙に書き出す。記憶だけでは忘れていることもあるので、再確認を含めて。そうすることで優先順位を付けたり、1つのことを時間内でやろうという目標になる。すべてのことが1日でできたら自分の自信につながり、上司からもできる奴という評価を得られ、一石二鳥になる。

Write out everything your boss has told you to do, as well as all tasks and appointments with confirmed dates and deadlines. You're going to forget if you just rely on your memory, so make sure to always double check. This way, you'll be able to order things according to priority, make sure to accomplish a certain task within the allocated time, and frame other concrete objectives. Not only will your self-confidence get a boost when you get everything done within a single day, you'll also make a great impression on your boss.

THURSDAY	FRIDAY	SATURDAY	SUNDAY
	31	1 休	**2** February 2014 如月 18' 生田スタジオ届 クランクアップ花束 宅間伸さん ¥3,000 AP菊ちせさん
指名 花束 st-by 火等資料作成 議事作成	7 市場(サンダーズパトル句) 8:30 角川大映画 クランクアップ花束 伊藤店 ¥2,000 AP久保田さん 16' LOGOS展示会 バラン大林 19:30~ 目黒届 フジフラワー ゼンタ系アレンジ ¥5,000 レンタル EASE 返却	8 休	9 st-by 8' ドリマオ社届 クランクアップ花束 ¥3,000 ドリマ塩オサムさん
~代々木体育館展示会 大花束 付箋張る st-by	14 市場(14.17.18日分) 10着 松井届 ワケありレッドゾーン受取込み 12届 イベント アレンジ 舞台メラキ 14届 ネイバーズワイフさん 花束副知 ¥4,200(税込) 大久保さん 14届 サンダーズさん 花束サトウ ¥2,000 小山さん 20着 ワケあり レッドゾーン バラン	15 夜のみ 花束 st-by 休	16 6:45届 ドリ次届 クランクアップ花束 ¥5,000 ドリマ田木さん
X① 未確認生物 (上) 19×2ケース AP吉良さん 映マツ西尾さん資料集め	21 市場(21日分) 10' 次映マツ 西尾さん (打) shoca st-by ↓ PM届 緑が丘 アレンジ ¥10,000 フジフラワー 20' shoca返却 未確認生物 19×2ケース AP吉良さん	22 高瀬 st-by ← 休	23 6:45届 ドリマオ社 クランクアップ花束 ¥3,000×2 ネイレ木村さん 8:40A 銀座 たかとし涙が止まらナイト 3列~本着 9届 久我山 クランクアップ花束 ¥3,000 ネイレ中村さん 21' 銀座 たかとしバラン再入
東st ストッグゼロCM 預かし 代官山展示会 虫st ストッグゼロCM バラン	28 AM ストッグゼロCM片付け st-by (打) 資料作成 ↓ 18:30 代々木公園 りっちゃん ウェディング (打)	3/1 PM届 TMC-A① コントの為劇場 → 16' 次町st 三田代バラン~ 建込み 20'~ LOGOSイオ装張 バラン	2
	7	8	9

自然に
障りなく
見せよう

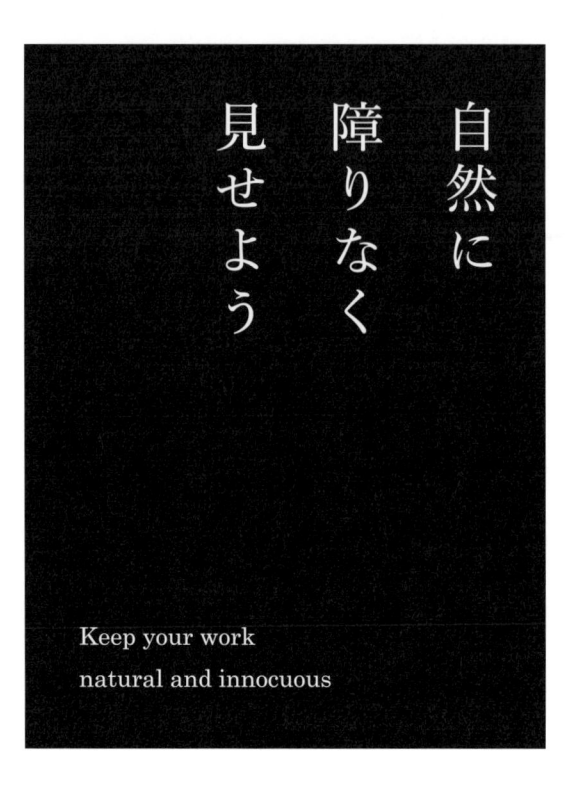

Keep your work
natural and innocuous

個人的、また恣意的なアウトプットは避ける。多くの既視感の集積で、障りのない作品はできている。一見自然に、かつ障りなく見えることにはけっこうな労力が払われている。

Avoid producing end results that are too individualistic or arbitrary. Unassuming work is the result of a prolonged, accumulated sense of déjà vu. Things that seem to have come about naturally, or which appear innocuous, often involve enormous amounts of time and labor.

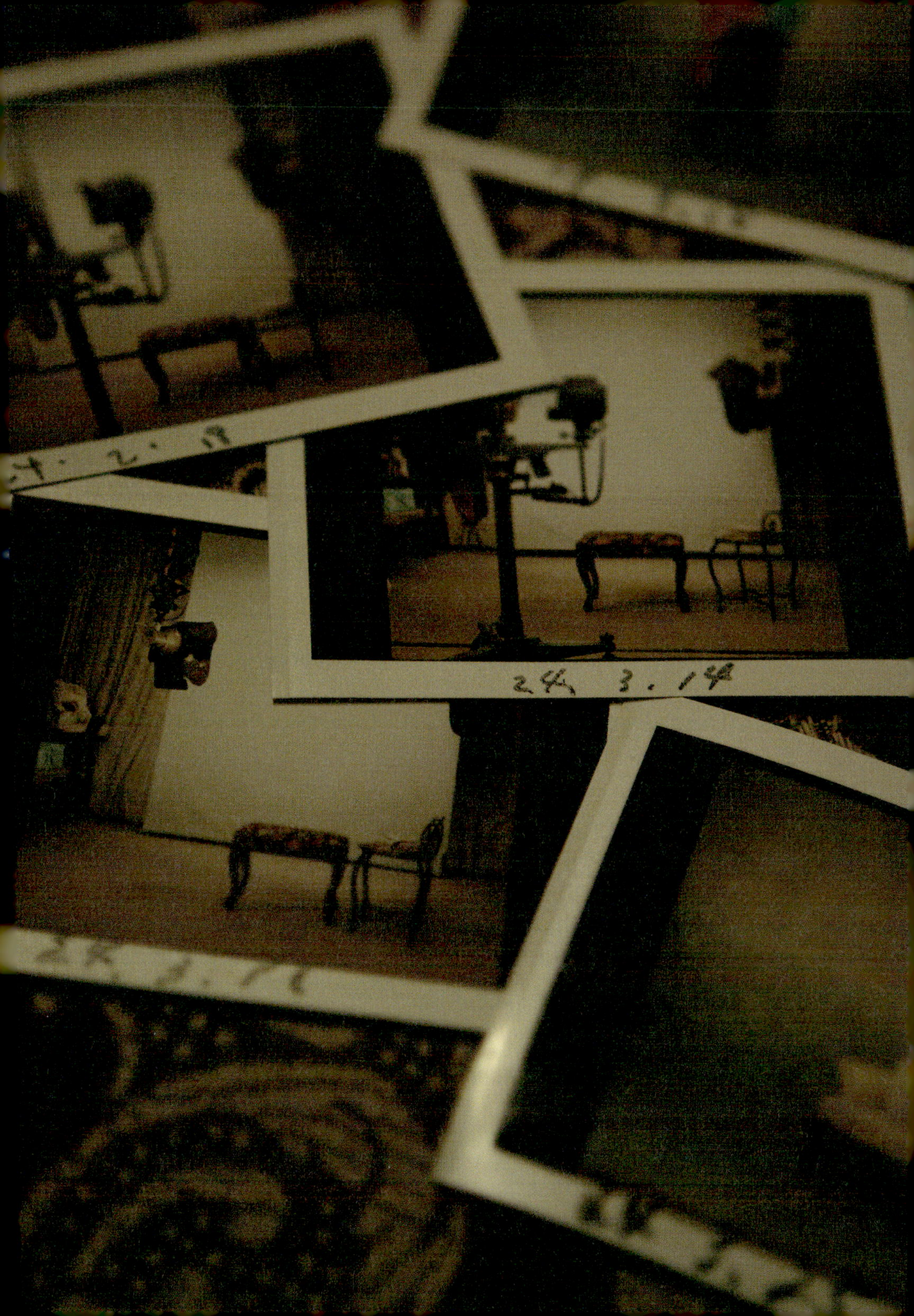
24 3.14

現場では歩き⊙ろう

Do your site recce

仕事の場には早めに同期同調したい。例えば写真撮影の現場では、その空間にチューニングできるよう、運動前の体操のようにまずはひたすら歩いている。流れが途切れないように撮影し続けることで、さらに合ってくる。空間になじみアングルも見慣れたものになり疲れてくるころ、いい加減さが顔を出し、それはそれでいいものが撮れる。こともある。

It's a good idea to get properly acquainted with the site you'll be working at as soon as possible. Walk around as if you were warming up before exercising in order to get in tune with the space. You'll synchronize even better with the location by shooting continuously, so that your "flow" won't be interrupted. When you start to tire of the familiar angles and objects within that space, a certain sloppiness will begin to show, and you can sometimes just shoot it that way.

225

先人の築いた価値を尊重しよう

Respect the values put in place
by those who came before you

先人が特定のジャンルを築いてきたおかげで、今の自分の仕事があるのだと考えること。例えば写真では、写真の価値、美的な基準、アングル、作法など。先人の築いた価値を侵さないように心がける。

You're able to pursue the work you do today thanks to the specific genres created by your predecessors. In the case of photography, this includes the values associated with the medium, aesthetic criteria, camera angles, and established protocols. Make sure you don't devalue the foundations that these people have built.

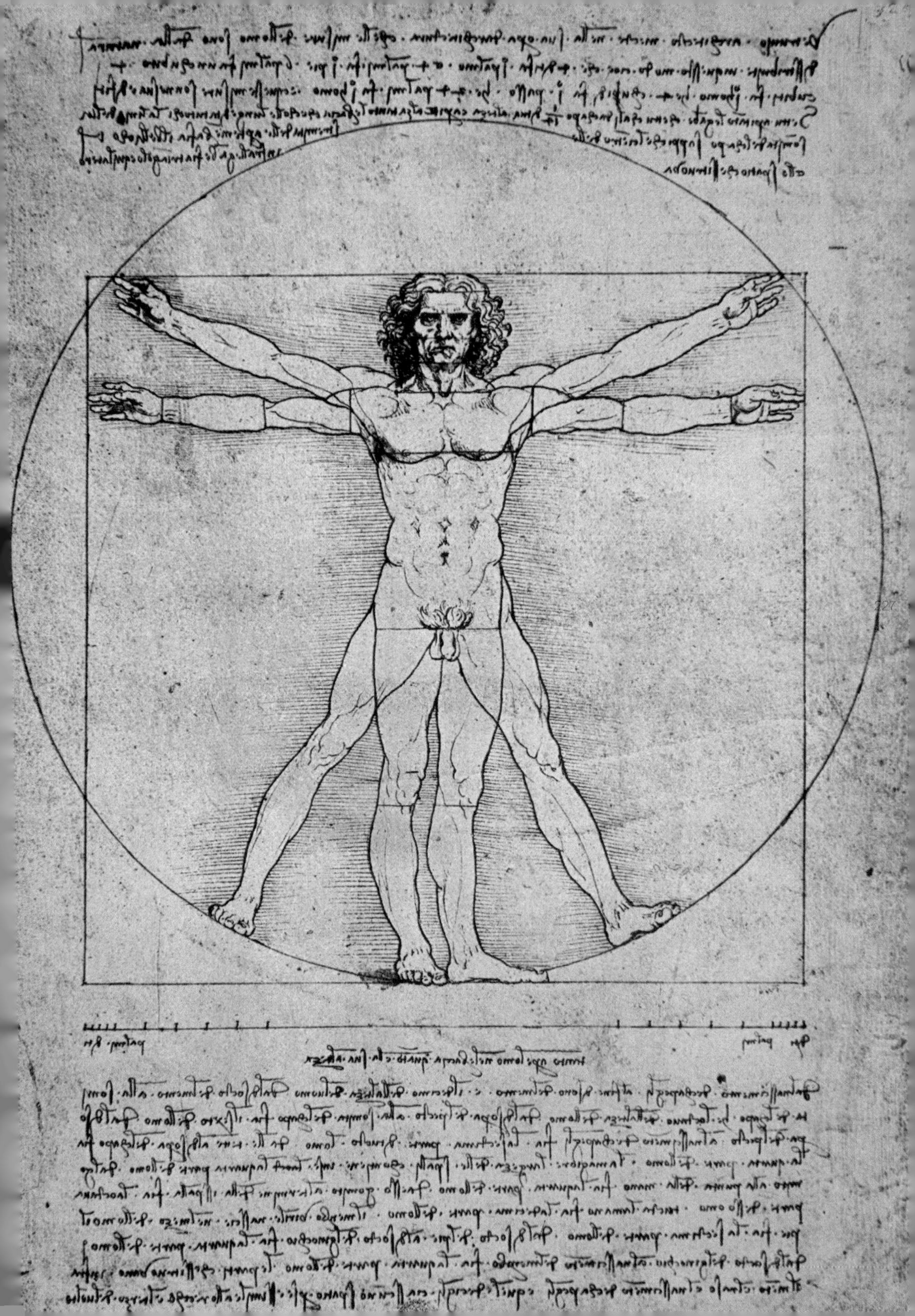

条件を味方に付けよう

Turn your circumstances to your advantage

仕事の条件はすべて外にあり、他人がつくったもの、その制約のなかからかたちを出すことが多い。さらに限られた時間内で成果を出すには、タイミングや工期、気象条件などで判断していくしかない。「受け身の功」とでもいうのだろうか。最大限の結果を残すためには、与条件をうまく味方に付けたい。

The conditions that govern your work all come from the outside. Typically, you're working to craft something out of the restrictions and limitations that arise from what other people have already put in place. In order to produce results within a limited time frame, you have no choice but to make decisions based on timing, the time period given to you, and the weather conditions involved — basically, working from a defensive or passive position. In order to have maximum impact, you need to turn the given circumstances to your advantage.

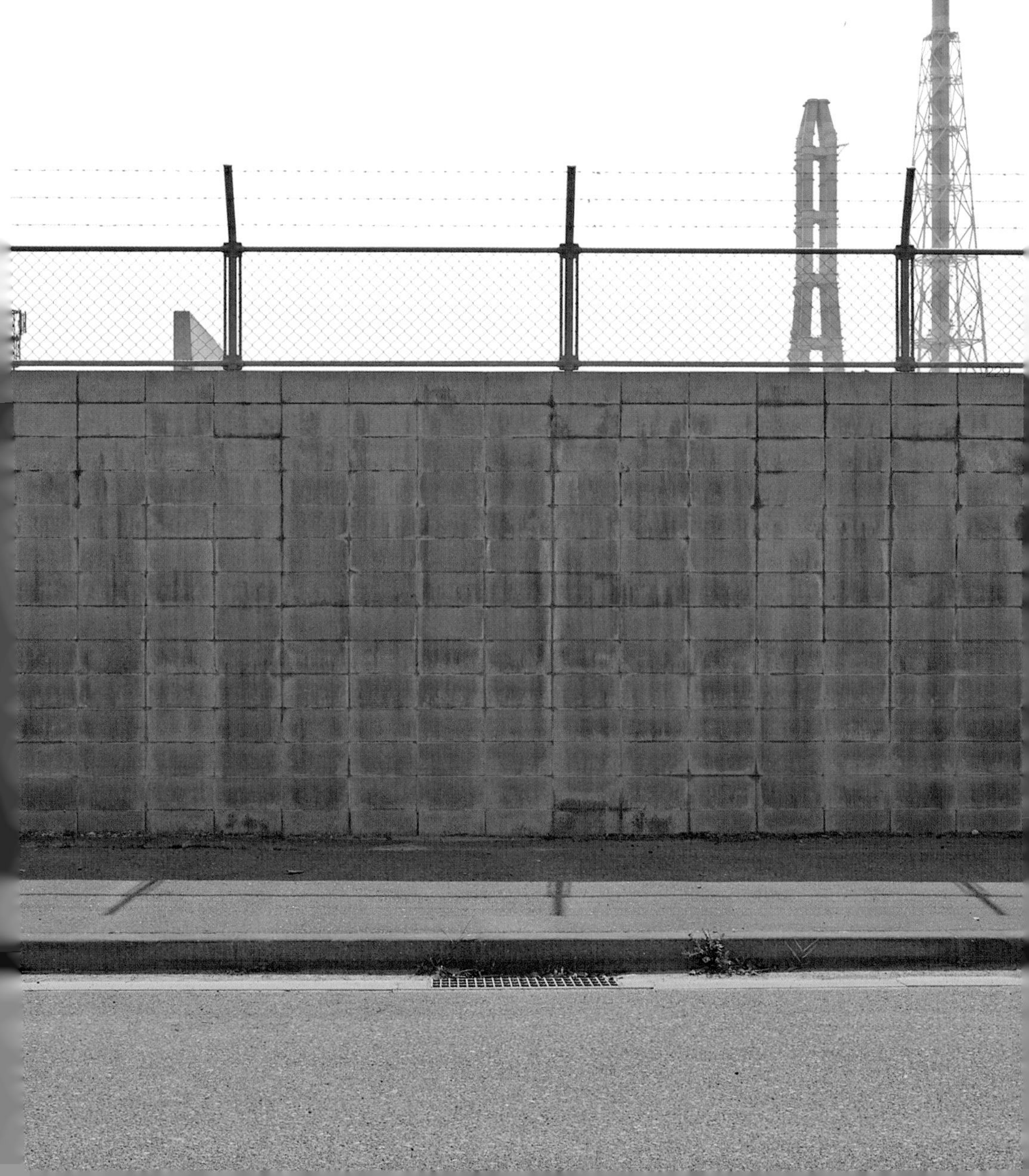

ピュアになろう

Keep your heart and mind pure

経験を積み、歳を重ねてからこそ意識的に純粋な目でものを見つめ、オープンマインドで物事に取り組もう。何事に対しても"慣れ"てしまわないように自分をもっていく。ダメ出ししてくれる人や怒ってくれる人には感謝。「まだまだこれから」という姿勢が、未来の自分や仕事の姿に直結していく。

Make a conscious decision to look at things with a clear mind unclouded by preconceptions after you've chalked up years of experience, and try to tackle things with an open mind. Don't let yourself "get used" to anything. Be grateful to nitpickers and those who get mad at you. Staying humble and modest about your own abilities will have a direct impact on how you develop in the future, and the work that you'll be capable of.

231

Keep to an ideal size

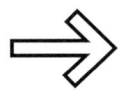

組織の
ほどよい → 規模を
考えよう

仕事のクオリティを維持する適正な組織の規模を見誤っては
いけない。人の数がある規模を超えた瞬間に、仕事のクオリ
ティが大きく下降するポイントがある。期待されている仕事
のクオリティを保つためには、その仕事の内容や管理者の能
力に見合った、適正な組織の規模を見つけなければならない。

Never misjudge the appropriate scale of the organization required to maintain the quality of your work. The moment the number of staff exceeds a certain limit, the standard of their work is going to nosedive. In order to maintain the quality of work expected, you need to find an ideal size and scale for your organization that corresponds with the content of the work and the abilities of your managers.

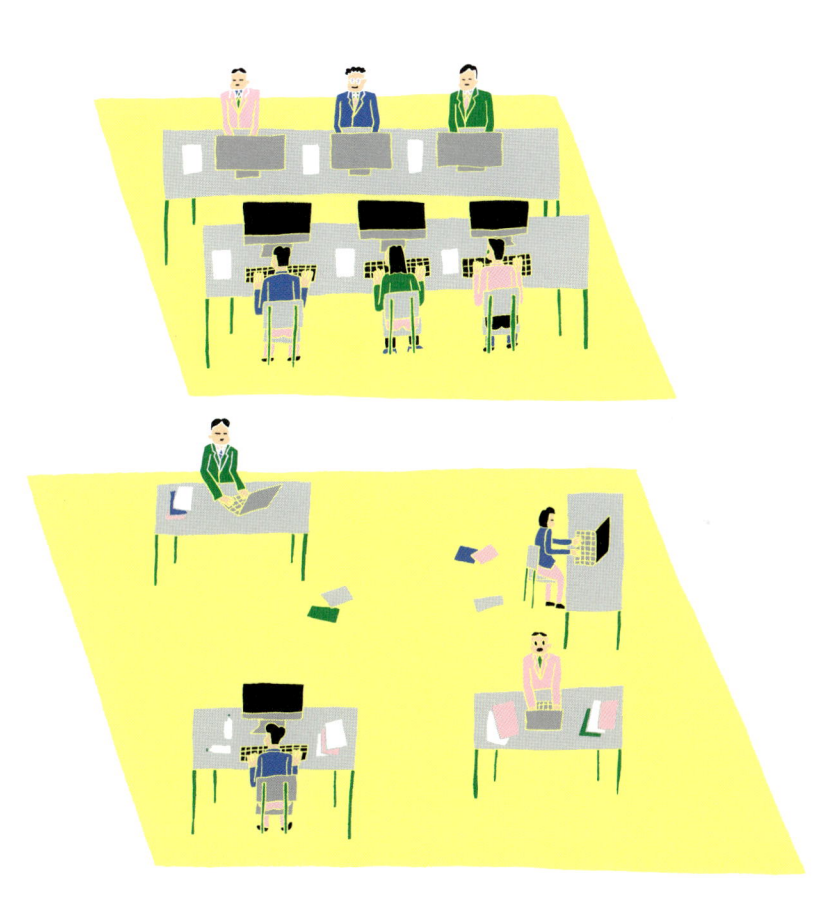

お金の意味を理解しよう

Understand the
meaning of money

「日本人は本当に人がいい」。国内では美徳になるが、海外のビジネスの場では馬鹿にした言葉になる。外国では、ビジネス＝金だ。自分が提示する金額＝自信の度合いである。高い見積もりを出したほうが評価される場面もあるぐらいだ。一方、無償でデザイン提案をすることは、食い逃げ犯を許すことである。レストランで「一番おいしかったらお金を払う」なんて言えるだろうか。そのことを承知のうえで、戦略的に覚悟を持って応じるのならばよい。

"Japanese are very nice." Even if it's a virtue in Japan, it is a contemptuous saying in international business situations. Overseas, business equals money. Your offering price shows your degree of confidence. Sometimes a more expensive offer is more highly-regarded. Meanwhile, proposing a design for free is like forgiving a person who eats and runs. Would you be able to say at a restaurant, "I'll only pay if the food is the best-tasting"? With this in mind, it is OK to respond strategically.

235

デザインを
生かし / 活かし
続けよう

Keep making good use of that design

デザインは作者の手を離れてしまうとコントロールできない。デザインを過去のものにするか、生き続けさせるかはデザイナー次第である。生かし、輝き続けさせるにはメンテナンスが必要であり、作品を活かすのはPRに委ねられるエリアでもある。作品は生まれたところがゴールではなく、その後もずっと勝負であるということを忘れないでいたい。

Creators lose control of their design once it leaves their hands. It's entirely up to the designer whether he consigns his design to the past, or decides to continue leveraging and making use of it. There's a lot of maintenance work that needs to be done so that your design continues to shine and be of use. Making continued use of that particular work is also something that you can entrust to your PR campaign. The ultimate goal shouldn't be the point at which the work comes into existence. Don't forget that your design needs to continue to excel long after that.

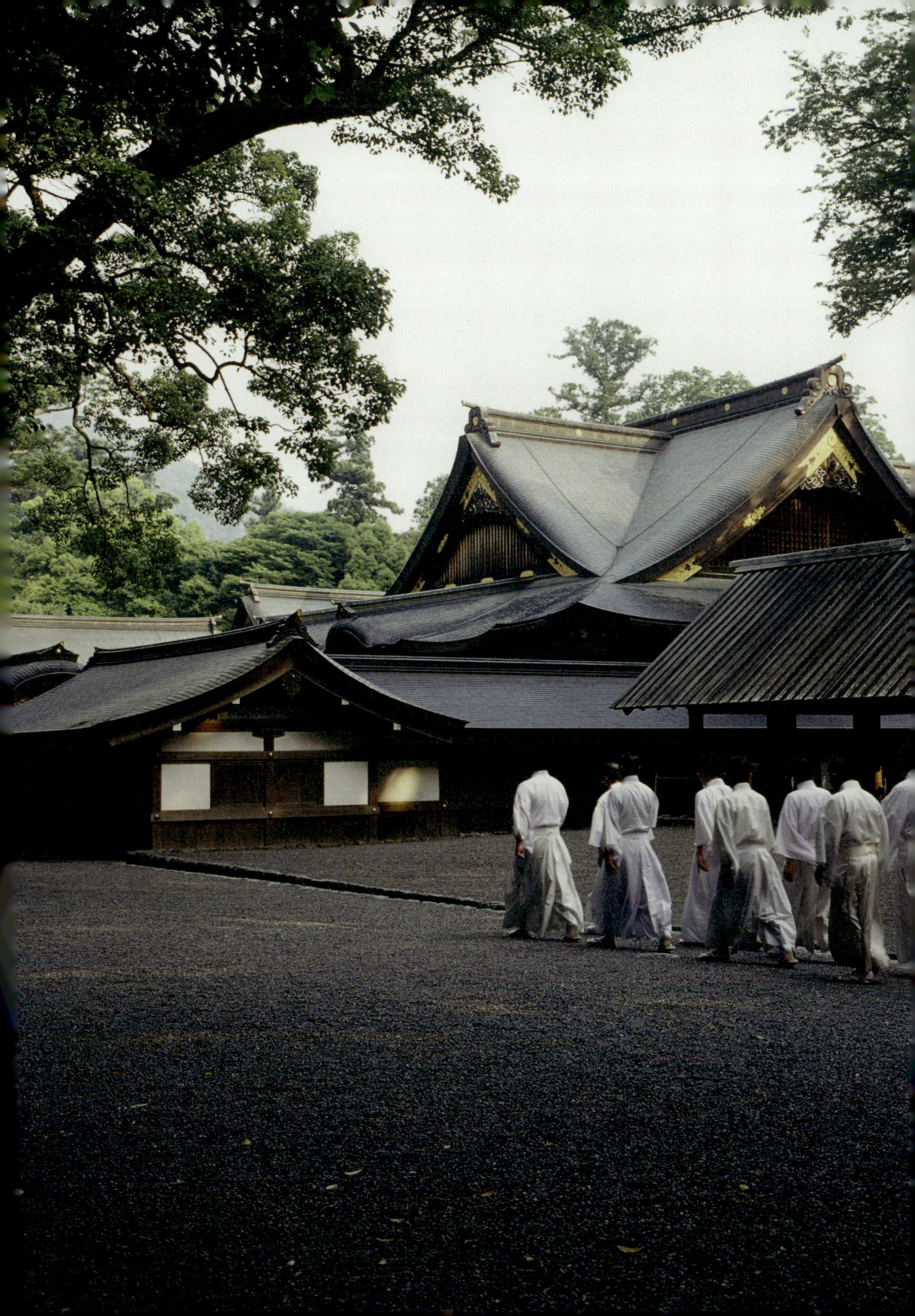

Past ◀┅┅ Take the long view ┅┅▶ Future

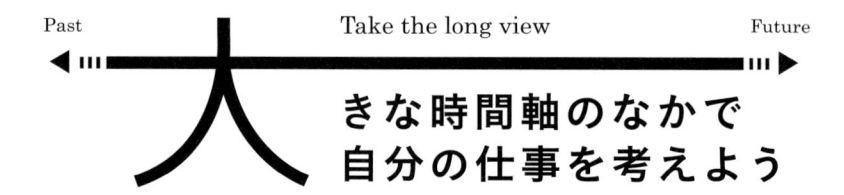

大きな時間軸のなかで自分の仕事を考えよう

どのような仕事であっても刹那的に捉えるのではなく、相手の過去の時間を引き継ぎ、未来へ送り出す仕事であると考えると意味が大きく変わる。不特定多数の人々に時間を超えて見られることもあるのだと想像すると、うかうかしてはいられない。

Whatever the job may be, don't think of it as a one-off, transient thing. The work takes on an entirely new meaning if you look at it as an extension of the time that the other person has already invested, and something that you offer up to the future. You won't be able to just sit around idly if you imagine all those eyes watching what you do, whether now or sometime in the future.

239

Happiness through the stomach

胃袋をつかめ

スタッフとの距離を縮めたいのであれば、まずはうまいモノをご馳走してあげることにつきる。おいしいゴハンをご馳走してくれる人によい印象をもつのは、人間の本能といっても過言ではない。そして、忘れてはいけないのは、その際によく話を聞き、褒めてあげること。つまり…、「恋愛」と一緒。

If you want to break the ice and bring your staff closer together, pull out all the stops and take them out for a fantastic dinner. It's only natural to have a good impression of someone who lavishes all that good food on you. And don't forget to listen to all their little stories and gossip and shower praise on them – just like you'd do with your lover, basically.

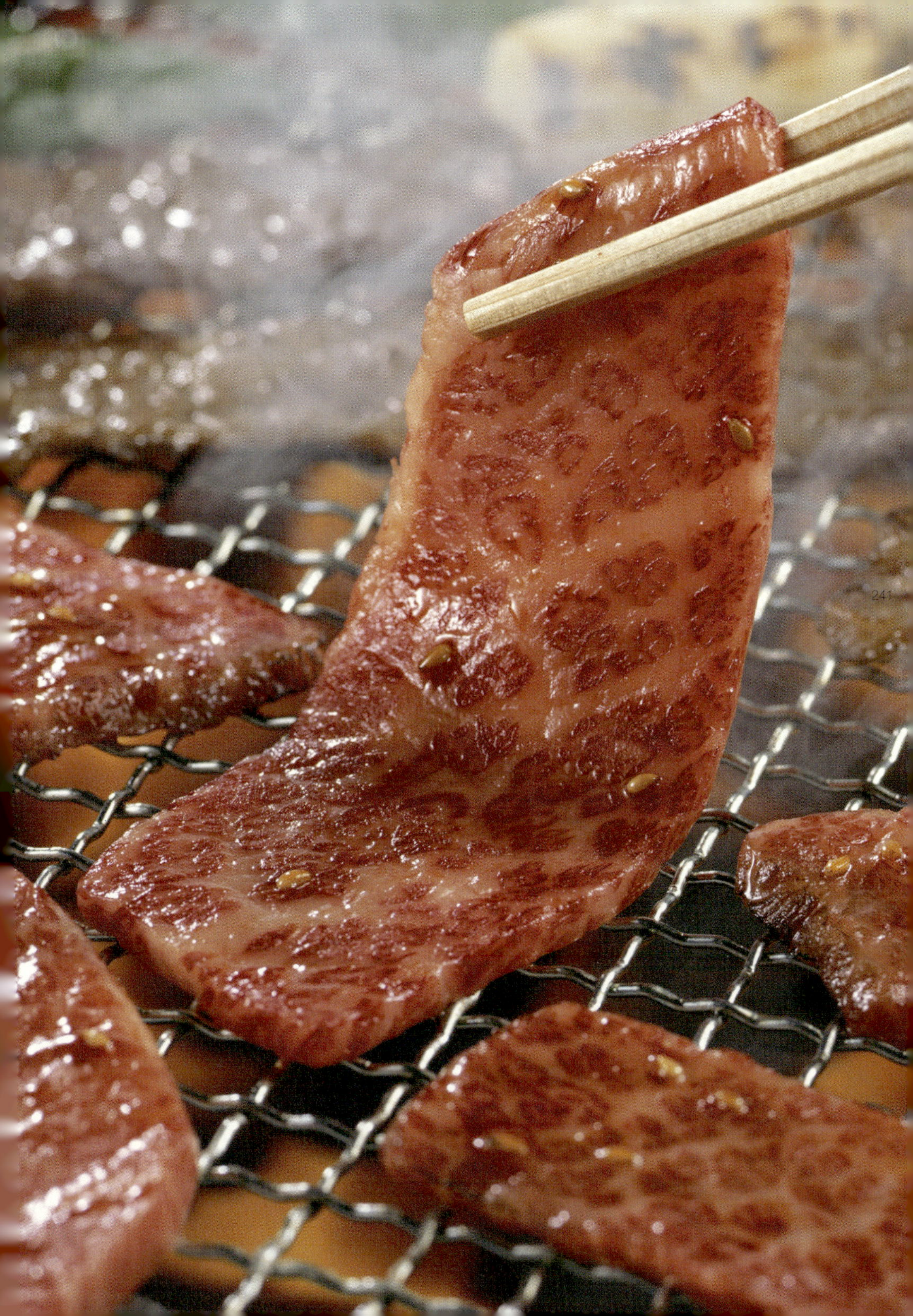

出版物の力で
次のステージへ進もう

Use the power of print to get to
the next level

有名になったデザイナーは、必ずといっていいほどキャリアの最初のほうで本を出したり有名雑誌に掲載され、それらの評価によってさらに認知されている。デザイン作業はとかく地味になりがち。出版物によって華やかさを得よう。社会からの信頼を得よう。出版社と仲よくなることは、デザイナーとして大変有効である。

Almost all the designers who went on to become famous published books early on in their careers and were featured in top magazines ⌐— which then helped them to win even more recognition. The actual work of design tends to be fairly low-key, so you should turn to paper media to chase the glory you've been looking for, and win some measure of trust and respect from the public. Getting friendly with publishers will give designers that extra edge.

腕のいい デザイナーが 必ずやっている 仕事のルール125

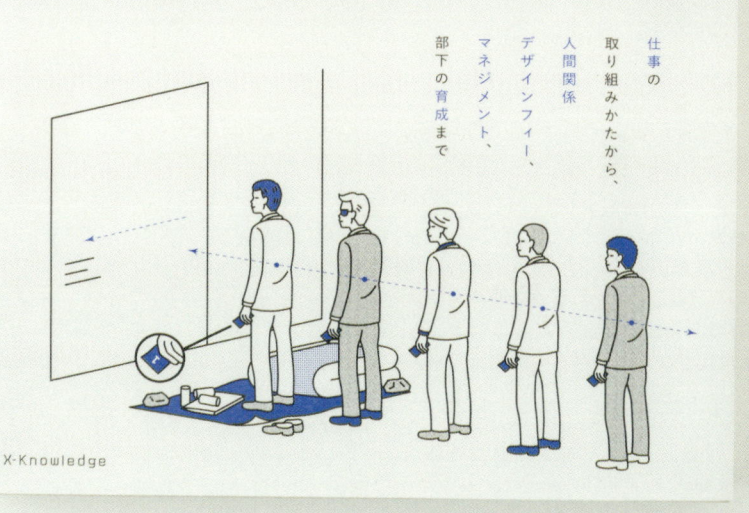

仕事の取り組みかたから、人間関係、デザインフィー、マネジメント、部下の育成まで

X-Knowledge

仕事を趣味にしない

Don't make your work your hobby

「趣味は仕事です！」そんなスタッフがいたら、即刻死刑。そんなスタッフを雇ってしまった経営者も、ハラキリ。だいたい趣味というのは余暇に行うものであり、道楽である。「今度、休暇がとれたら仕事しよっと！」 道楽感覚で仕事をされては、たまったものではない。

If any of your staff tells you that their hobby is their work – off with their head! The manager who hired the guy ought to be done away with, too. A hobby is something you enjoy at leisure during your down time, for recreation or amusement. "The next time I get a free moment, I'm going to get some work done!" Being made to slog away for fun is simply inexcusable.

レジとです…

ごしゅみは〜

思いがけず

あいた

時間

を有効に

活用しよう

Make good use of
unexpected free time

忙しくないときの時間の使い方が重要である。仕事がたくさんあって、それを忙しくこなしていくことは誰にでもできる。仕事を長く続けていくために重要なのは、仕事がぽっかりとなくなった時間の乗り切り方だ。

Be careful how you allocate your time when you're not that busy. Anyone can attend frantically to a heavy workload when the going gets tough. What you really need to know in order to carry on working over the long haul is how to get through those times when the work just completely dries up.

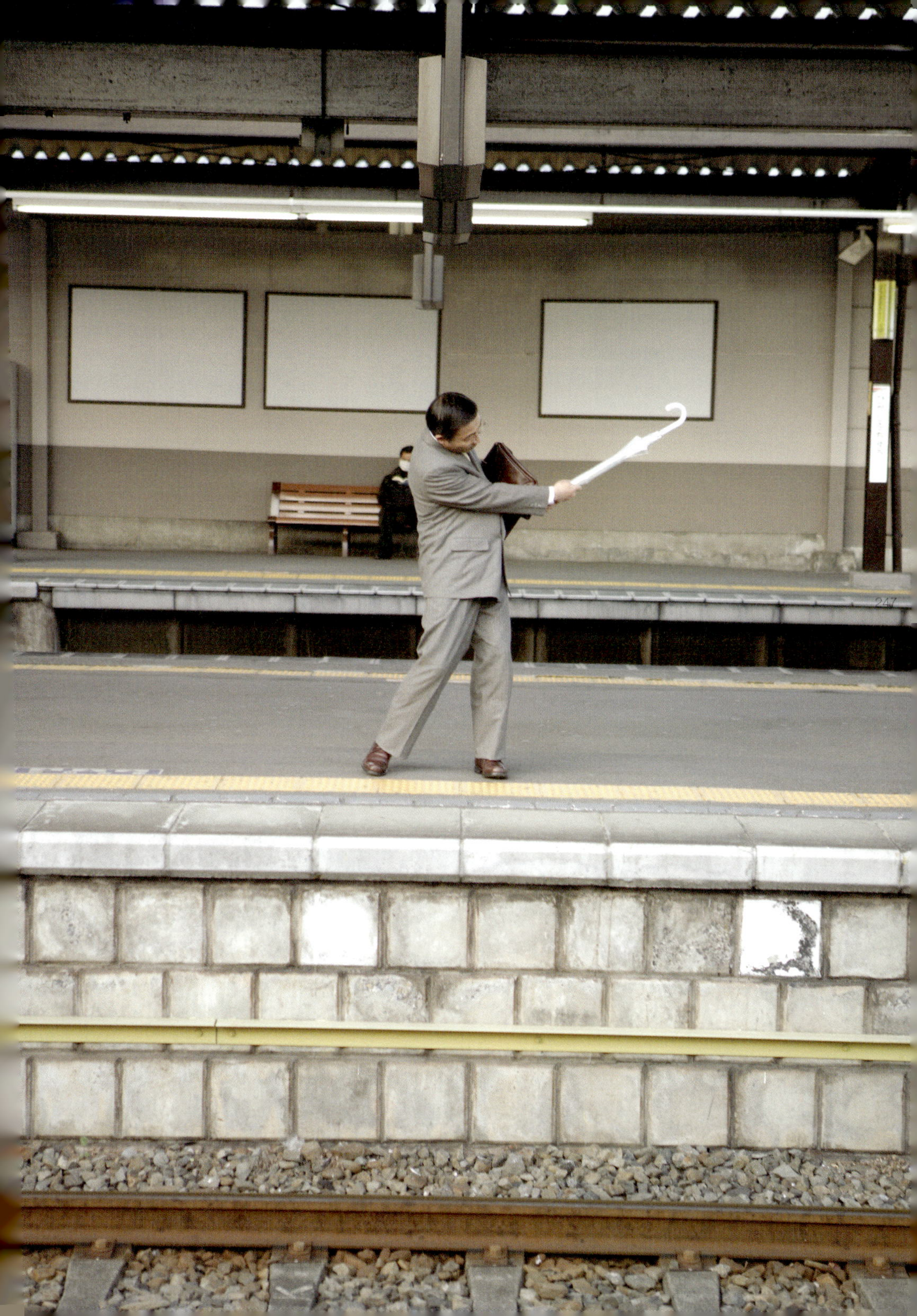

プレッシャーを"喜び"に変えよう

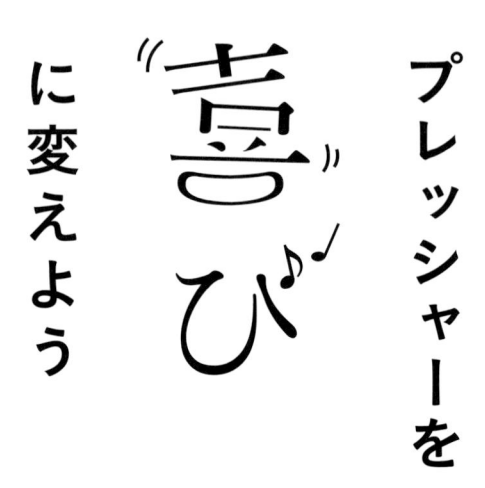

Convert pressure to pleasure

デザイン業は常にプレッシャーを背負い続ける宿命にある。だって自分だって何が答えか分からないときに制限時間付きで仕事を依頼されるのだから。デザインで身を立てるなら、プレッシャーの苦しさを喜びに変える技を身に着けるしかない。プレッシャーは期待の裏返し。期待されないよりは、期待されているほうが幸せでしょう？ なんとかして喜ばせたい、と思えるようになったらデザイナーとして合格だ。

Design work is destined to produce constant pressure, since you get a work offer with a deadline but you don't have an answer. To make a living by designing, you must learn techniques to convert the agony of pressure into pleasure. Pressure is the flip side of the client's expectations. Isn't it better to have high expectations for you than to not? When you can think of how to provide pleasure, you are a full-fledged designer.

PRESSURE

前向きさを引き継いで
仕事の原動力としよう

Turn your optimism into a motivating force

仕事の前提がポジティブな始まりであるといい。結婚式、七五三、旅行記念など写真はうれしい出来事と結びついている。それは建築の写真においても同じで、きれいなものを永遠に美しく残したいというポジティブな前提がある。その時を共有しながらも、写真はその建築の未来の顔として動き始めるという怖さも同時に見ていなくてはならない。

The premise of your work is that these photos will be the start of something big. We associate photographs with happy events and occasions, like weddings and vacations. The same is true of architectural photography — it exists because we want to create an aesthetically pleasing record of these beautiful buildings for posterity. Although your work serves to share this particular moment with other people, you also need to be aware of the slightly frightening fact that these images are going to become a future document of these architectural works.

想像力を働かせよう

Fire up your imagination

海外から突然メールがきて、仕事やコラボレーションの依頼が入ることも珍しくない時代。電話やメールのみで仕事が始まったり終わったり。英語が母国語でない者同士、時にすれ違い、悔しい想いをすることもある。でもそこで諦めたらおしまい。テレポーテーションするかのように相手の立場で考えてみる。ニュアンスから想像力をフルに働かせれば、世界中の人と関わることは難しくない。

These days, it's not uncommon for an email from a foreign client to suddenly appear in your inbox with an offer of work or a proposal to collaborate. Projects can get off the ground or shelved just through the telephone or email. It can be an utterly frustrating experience when misunderstandings occur among people whose first language is not English – but once you give up, that's the end of the story. Try putting yourself in the other person's shoes and thinking about things from their point of view – just as if you'd teleported yourself next to them. Fire up your imagination and decode those nuances, and you'll find that it's not such a stretch to communicate with people from all over the world.

تحية طيبة وبعد..

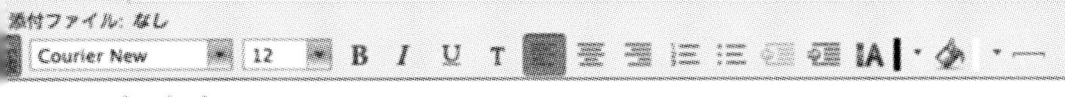

اسمحوا لنا أن نقدم لكم شركتنا التي تعمل في مجال التصميم والتحرير والكتابة. وتختص في تصميم وتخطيط الكتب والمجلات والنشرات والمطبوعات الإعلانية عن طريق النشر المكتبي (DTP)

عرفنا على شركتكم الموقرة بعد أن رأينا موقعكم على الانترنت، وسيكون لنا جزيل الشرف إذا وافقتكم على التعاون معنا عن طريق تعهيد جزء من أعمالكم لشركتنا

نعلم تماماً قدر إنشغالكم بأعمالكم كثيرة، ولكن سنكون في غاية الامتنان إذا تكرمتم بتحديد موعد للمقابلة حتى نشرح لسيادتكم كافة التفاصيل الخاصة بشركتنا

نشكركم على اهتمامكم بهذا الأمر وفي إنتظار ردكم لتحديد موعد للمقابلة

وتفضلوا بقبول فائق التحية والاحترام

デザイン以外をデ゛ザ゛イ゛ン゛しよう

Design something other
than the product itself

いくらすばらしい成果を出せたとしても、そのプロセスやあなたの人柄もクライアントは見ていることを忘れないで。よい成果は当たり前。成果が同じでも、何で差をつけるか？それをデザインできてこそ、真のデザイナーといえる。

No matter how great a job you manage to do, never forget that your clients have their eyes on the entire process, and your own personality. Clients expect great results as a bare minimum. If the end product is the same, what's going to make the difference? Only when you manage to "design" these other aspects of your practice can you call yourself a real designer.

A B C D E F G
H I J K L M N
O P Q R S T U
V W X Y Z

古くならない ものに 新しさを 見出そう

Discover newness in things that don't get old

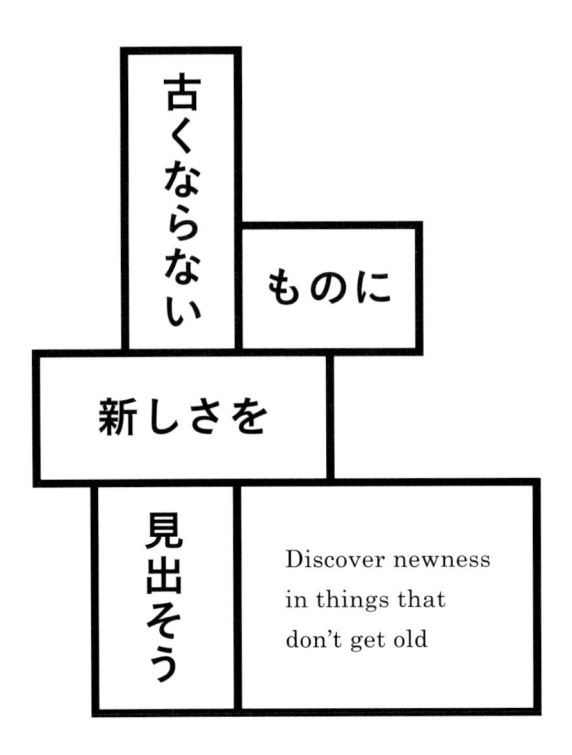

　新しさを生み出すことができるのは、人が気付かないことにいち早く気付いたり、世のなかにないものを予見したり、仮想したりする能力があるからである。ほかと異なる目新しい何かを見出そうとする行為がデザイン本来の価値ではないから、そのことに必要以上に強迫観念を抱いてはならない。新しさは目の前にもたくさん存在しており、その組み合わせ次第でいくらでも新しさは生み出せる。古くならないものこそが、唯一新しいデザインである。

Being able to produce something new is really about the ability to realize quickly what others haven't, to foresee things that haven't appeared yet, or to have a certain hypothetical, imaginative vision. Discovering something new and original that is different from everything else out there is not what design is good for, so you shouldn't obsess over that more than necessary. There are lots of new, fresh things are right there in front of you. All the originality and newness you want are yours for the taking, as long as you combine these things in the right way. Things that don't get old are the only "new designs" there are.

257

情報はクリアであれ

Make information clear

あなたのことを知りたい人は、何よりもわかりやすい情報を求めている。格好のよいウェブサイトや、難しいコンセプトを連ねたポートフォリオをつくる必要はない。簡潔なメッセージ、わかりやすい記載。そして、アップデートを怠らないでいるだけで事務所はぐっとPR体質になる。

People who want to know more about you are looking for information that's easy to understand, more than anything else. You don't need a fancy website or portfolio with a complex concept in tow. What matters is a simple, concise message and clear-cut presentation. Just by not being lazy with updates, your firm is going to get a solid PR boost.

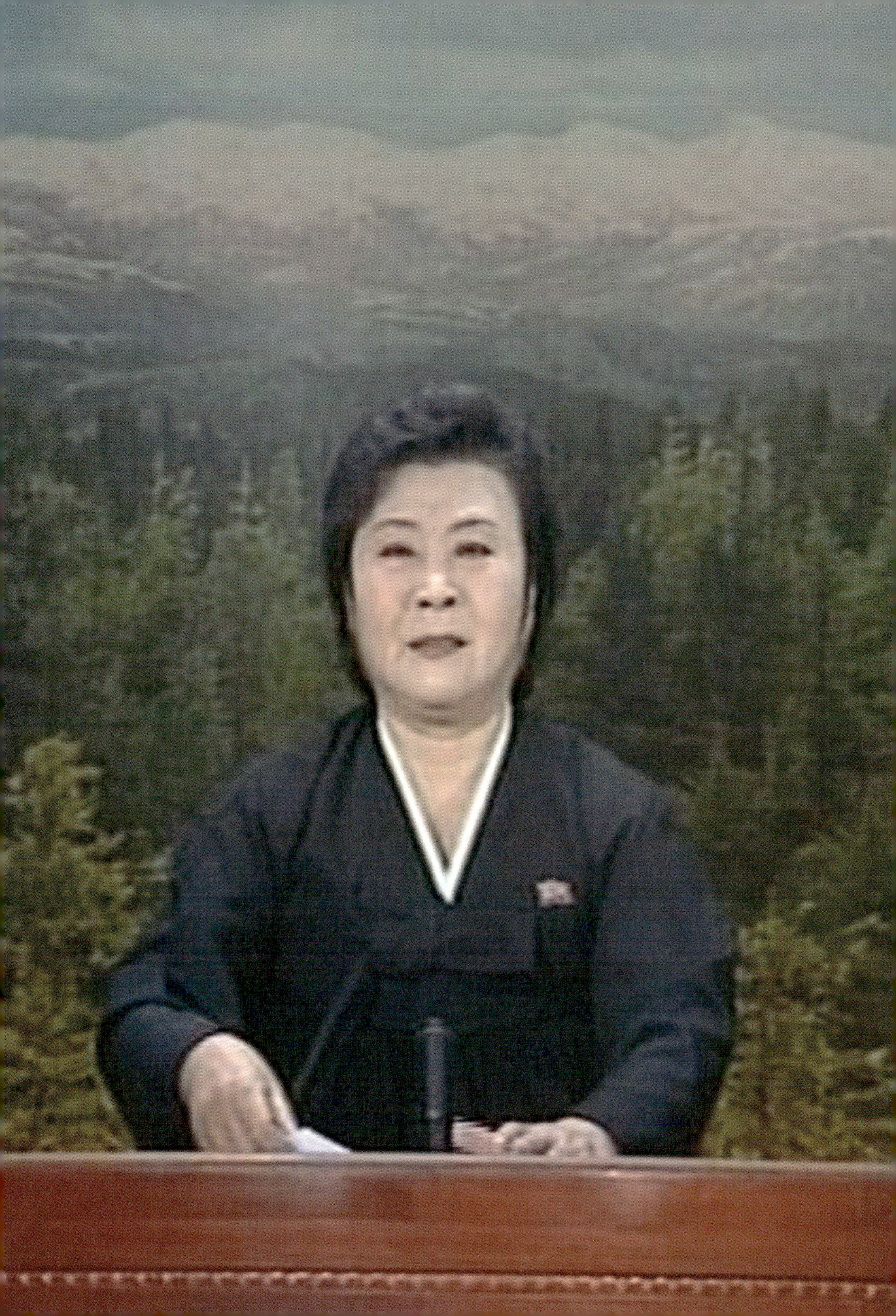

顔を見せ合う仕事をしよう

Face time is important

相手の顔が見えることで、仕事での人から1人の個人だという気持ちが入ってくる。個人性が垣間見られると、仕事が仕事以上のものに思えてきて、相手の仕事を自分事として引き受けられる。

You learn to appreciate your clients and colleagues as individuals by interacting with them face to face. When you get a glimpse of what it is that makes people unique, work will stop being just work, and other people's work will become something personal to you, too.

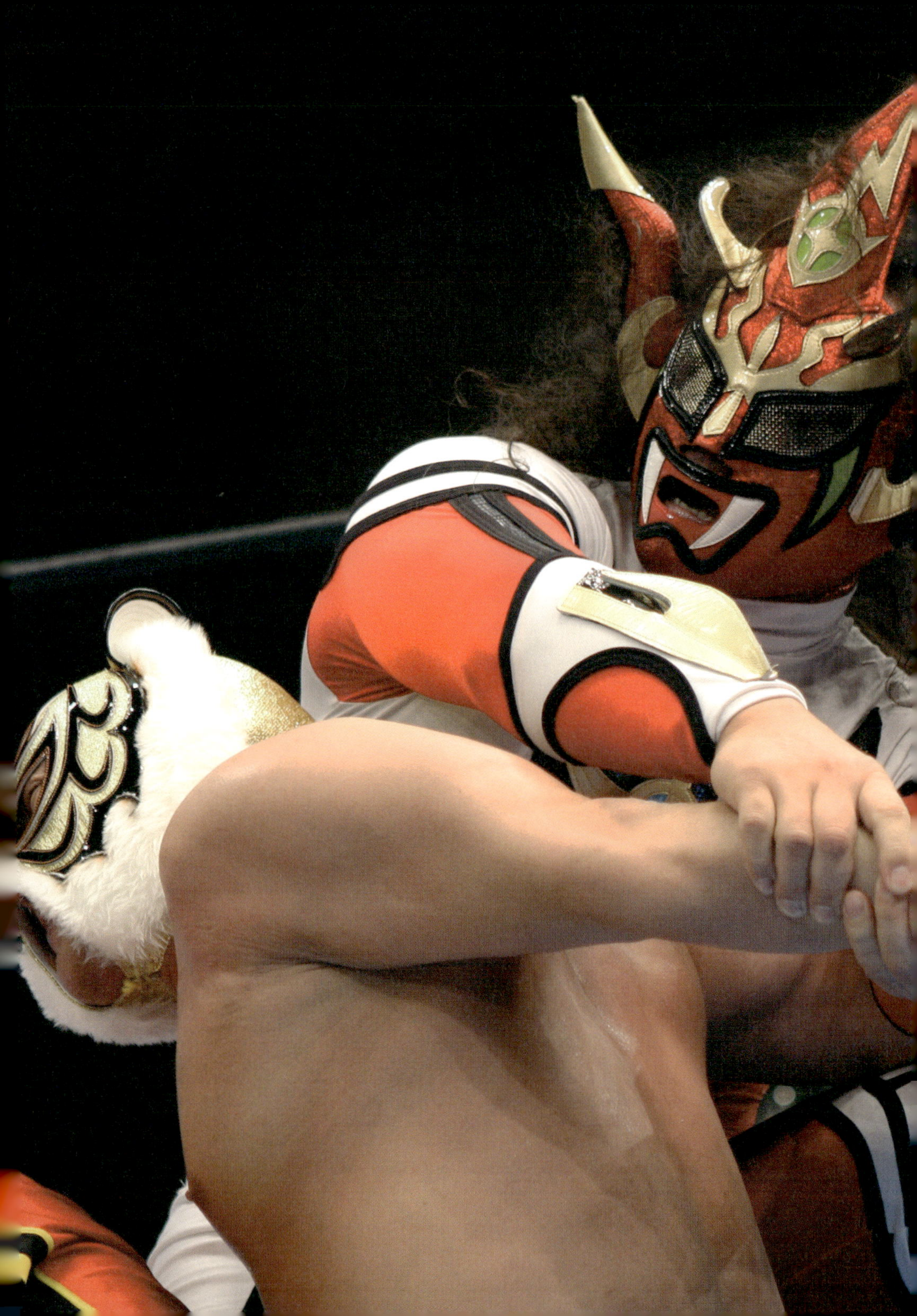

Start　　　　　　　　　　Time limit　　　　　　　　Delivery

時間を寸ろう

Keep to the schedule

時間をかければ、よりよいものができる、よいデザインになる。これは本当だろうか？お仕事でモノをつくる／デザインする場合は必ず発注者がいるし、その発注者は売り時を考慮して販売計画を立てているはず。時間を守ること、時間内にモノをつくることも重要なことである。

Spending more time will lead you to a better end product and design. Is that really true? People who make or design things for a living necessarily work for clients or outsourcers who have undoubtedly drawn up a sales plan that takes into account when the product will hit the market. Working on schedule and producing results within the stipulated time are also important.

託 銀
場 行
所

三井信

23
下馬一丁目

著名な人ほどさん付けで呼ぼう

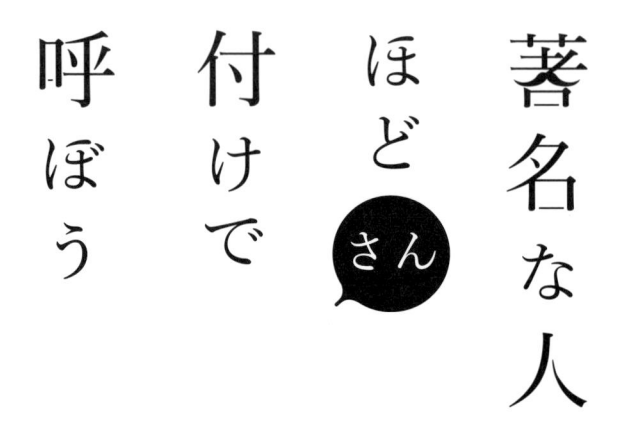

Pay more respect the more famous the person is

有名デザイナーの名前には「さん」を付けて会話しよう。会ったこともない有名なデザイナーについて会話のなかで引用するとき、例えば「安藤忠雄がさ〜」などと言ってはいけない。呼び捨てにしているうちは、あなたは決して安藤さんと同じ土俵に立てることはない。

When referring to famous designers in conversation, make sure to call them "-san". Never refer simply to "Tadao Ando" or other well-known designers whom you haven't even met without using an honorific. You'll never join the same league as Ando-san as long as you refer to him like that.

265

Q. 素晴らしい問いをつくろう
Ask great questions

A. _____

ものごとへの好奇心こそが、オリジナルの問いをつくり出す原動力である。決して答えではなく、いかに領域の広い問いをつくることができるかがデザインの力量であり、その問いに向かい合うことこそがモノづくりの醍醐味。素晴らしい問いの答えは、必ず素晴らしい。

Curiosity is a measure of your passion for coming up with creative and original questions. The power of design lies not in the answers it can proffer, but rather in how it can ask broad, all-encompassing questions about a particular domain. The real pleasure of making things comes from confronting these questions. The answers to great questions are necessarily going to be great, too.

このはし
わたる
べからず

PROFILE

宇野昇平 SHOHEI UNO
アートディレクター

P. 38, 86, 92, 116, 196, 240, 244, 254

1970年東京都生まれ。'95年日本大学大学院理工学研究科卒業後、建設コンサルタント/デザイン事務所を経て、SURMOMETER INC.を設立。土木/建築からファッション、フードなど、ジャンルや媒体を問わずPR、広告、ツール類の企画、書籍の監修などを行う。その傍ら「工藝うつわと道具SML」のバイヤー/ディレクターも務める。

喜多幸宏 YUKIHIRO KITA
編集者・プロデューサー

P. 30, 66, 108, 138, 160, 180, 188, 200, 262

1972年愛知県生まれ。文系の学部を卒業後、出版社を経て、フリー。建築から食など幅広いジャンルで、企画やプロデュースなどを行う。

木村 茂 SHIGERU KIMURA
不動産コンサルタント

P. 56, 80, 84, 94, 134, 150, 174, 178
232, 246, 264

東京都生まれ。1989年早稲田大学法学部卒業後、CIコンサルティング会社（PAOS）などを経て、2000年トランジスタ設立、代表取締役。宅地建物取引主任者、住宅ローンアドバイザー、公認不動産コンサルティングマスター。建築家のパートナーとして、デザインマインドのある不動産のコンサルティング、仲介、ファイナンスアドバイスを行う。

國時 誠 MAKOTO KUNITOKI
ファッションデザイナー

P. 54, 152, 156, 172, 194, 202, 208

1975年群馬県生まれ。2001年武蔵野美術大学造形学部空間演出デザイン学科 ファッションコース卒業。すべてが一点物「ボーダーシリーズ」が特徴的なファッションブランド「STORE」主宰。舞台衣裳も手がけるほか、日本各地で衣服をテーマとしたワークショップやアート展を開催、また地域密着型アートプロジェクト「TERATOTERA」のディレクターを務めるなど、多岐にわたり活動を展開している。

黒崎 敏 SATOSHI KUROSAKI
建築家

P. 12, 14, 16, 20, 26, 28, 34, 76, 96, 98
102, 104, 110, 112, 126, 130, 154, 158, 164
166, 168 176, 216, 256, 266

1970年石川県金沢市生まれ。'94明治大学理工学部建築学科卒業後、メーカー、設計事務所勤務を経て2000年APOLLO一級建築士事務所設立、現在代表取締役。慶應義塾大学大学院理工学研究科非常勤講師。住宅や商業を中心に国内外を問わず設計、コンサルティングを行う。GOOD DESIGN AWARD、東京建築賞、日本建築家協会優秀建築選など受賞多数。主な著書に『新しい住宅デザインの教科書』『最高に楽しい家づくりの図鑑』（共にエクスナレッジ）、『可笑しな家』『夢の棲み家』（二見書房）

戸恒浩人 HIROHITO TOTSUNE

照明デザイナー

P. 18, 24, 32, 40, 72, 82, 88, 100, 118, 124
128, 144, 234, 248

1975年生まれ。東京都出身。'97年東京大学工学部建築学科卒業後、ライティングプランナーズアソシエーツ（LPA）を経て、2005年シリウスライティングオフィス設立。建築・環境照明そして都市計画に至る豊富な経験を生かし、ジャンルを問わず活躍の場を広げている。東京スカイツリーをはじめ国内のさまざまな建築の照明を手掛けるほか、海外の大型建築の実績も多い。'13年北米照明学会・照明デザインアワードで最優秀賞を受賞。

鳥村鋼一 KOICHI TORIMURA

フォトグラファー

P. 46, 50, 52, 58, 62, 74, 148, 170, 192, 206
210 218, 222, 224, 226, 228, 238, 250, 260

1976年千葉県生まれ。'99年明治大学理工学部卒業後、ナカサ・アンド・パートナーズを経て、2007年鳥村鋼一写真事務所設立、主宰。住宅から商業建築、公共施設まで空間を撮り続け、建築家からの信頼も厚い。

藤原佐知子 SACHIKO FIJIWARA

flower decorator

P. 60, 142, 186, 190, 220

千葉県生まれ。私立高校を卒業後、フジテレビでお花装飾を経て、株式会社渚華-shoca-設立、代表取締役。生花はもちろんのこと造花、クリスマスやオブジェなどを装飾するほか、インテリアのスタイリングも行う。

武藤智花 CHIKA MUTO

建築デザイン専門PR

P. 6, 10, 42, 44, 78, 90, 120, 132, 146
162, 184, 230, 236, 242, 252, 258

武蔵野美術大学卒業後、クライン ダイサム アーキテクツにて広報・オフィスマネージャー・イベントコーディネーターなど建築家のサポートに従事。2006年建築家・デザイナーを対象に海外コミュニケーションやPRをサポートするネオプラシックステンを設立、主宰。

渡邊謙一郎 KUNICHIRO WATANABE

STANDARD TRADE. 代表

P. 8, 22, 36, 48, 64, 68, 70, 106, 114, 122
136, 140, 182, 198, 204, 212, 214

1972年横浜育ち。神奈川大学建築学科を卒業後、家具製作の道へ入り品川職業訓練校卒業。シンプルで良質な家具を一般住宅にも届けるために'98年STANDARD TRADE.を設立。以後、オリジナル家具のデザインから製造販売のほか、高い技術と空間バランスを評価され、住宅やオフィス店舗も手がけている。数々の著名な家具の修理・修覆・復元も手がけていることも評価されている。

写真	鳥村鋼一 P. 53, 63, 149, 193, 207, 219, 223, 229, 239, 251
	西川公朗 P. 97, 111, 151, 257
	高野尚人 P. 29, 133, 143, 189, 243
	Getty Images P. 9, 11, 25, 35, 39, 43, 45, 47, 49, 51, 69, 73, 79, 83, 87, 119, 147, 153, 157, 167, 181, 209, 213, 225, 231, 235
	amanaimages P. 17, 21, 41, 55, 57, 59, 61, 65, 67, 71, 77, 81, 109, 123, 137, 145, 161, 171, 177, 179, 185, 187, 195, 199, 227, 237, 241, 247, 263
	ピクスタ P. 27, 115, 155, 215
	小谷田整/アフロ P.31　Newscom/アフロ P.33　築田純/アフロスポーツ P.85 読売新聞/アフロ P.89, 117, 169, 197, 211　日刊スポーツ/アフロ P.95 AP/アフロ P.103　DUOMO Photography/アフロ P.107　Fortean/アフロ P.125 丹羽修/アフロ P.139　松岡健三郎/アフロ P.141　中村吉夫/アフロ P.175 Asia Images/アフロ P.191　Splash/アフロ P.203　川北茂貴/アフロ P.205 ロイター/アフロ P.259　平工幸雄/アフロ P.261　毎日新聞社/アフロ P.265
翻訳	武藤智花（ネオプラシックステン）
デザイン・DTP	宇野昇平、五木田裕之（surmometer inc.）
イラスト	小寺 練（surmometer inc.）
編集協力	加藤 純（context）

腕のいいデザイナーが
必ずやっている仕事のルール125

2014年4月1日　初版第1版発行
2014年12月10日　　第2刷発行

著者　　　宇野昇平、木村 茂、國時 誠、黒崎 敏、戸恒浩人、
　　　　　鳥村鋼一、藤原佐知子、武藤智花、渡邊謙一郎

発行者　　澤井聖一

発行所　　株式会社エクスナレッジ
　　　　　〒106-0032 東京都港区六本木7-2-26
　　　　　http://www.xknowledge.co.jp/

問い合せ先　編集 Tel：03-3403-1381　Fax：03-3403-1345　info@xknowledge.co.jp
　　　　　　販売 Tel：03-3403-1321　Fax：03-3403-1829

無断転載の禁止
本誌掲載記事（本文、図表、イラストなど）を当社および著作権者の承諾なしに無断で転載（翻訳、複写、データベースへの入力、インターネットでの掲載など）することを禁じます。